REINTERPRETING AMERICAN HISTORY

Reinterpreting American History

A Critical Look at Our Past

by

EDWARD DIENER

PHILOSOPHICAL LIBRARY
New York

Published by PHILOSOPHICAL LIBRARY, INC.,
15 East 40 Street, New York, N. Y. 10016.
Copyright 1975 by Edward Diener.
All rights reserved.

Library of Congress Catalog Card Number 75-378
SBN 8022-2166-1.

Manufactured in the United States of America.

DEDICATED TO MY PARENTS,
WHO TAUGHT ME TO LOVE HISTORY

TABLE OF CONTENTS

INTRODUCTION

America. The morning newspaper describes in horrifying detail the slaying of eight persons by a sniper from atop a New Orleans hotel. Young couples go on a date to see the erotic movie "Deep Throat." Male singer Alice Cooper savagely cuts up a child's doll to entertain his audience, and ends his show by pretending to hang himself. People in large cities breathe befouled air. Millions are unemployed. Of those who do work, many have dehumanizingly boring jobs which offer no opportunity for self-fulfillment. Old people on pensions literally cannot afford to eat. Citizens are stunned and confused when criminal acts are traced to the White House. The war in Southeast Asia continues with 10,000 or more American "advisers" on the scene.

The richest and most powerful nation on earth ridden with crime, pollution, poverty and moral corruption. What happened to America as she once was? What happened to the America of clean and bustling cities, poor men working hard on their way to wealth, an upright and God-fearing land? To the great country which stood for democracy and freedom around the globe? The answer is that *such an America never existed.*

America is not and never was Camelot. America is a powerful country plagued with uncountable problems. She was not always powerful, but her problems and mistakes have always been with her. Unfortunately most of us have been "brainwashed" to believe in America's pristine past by standard histories which offer a rose-colored version of the American past

9

which has little correspondence to fact. The truth is the first casualty here.

One purpose of this book is to demythologize United States history, to shed light on America's blunders and immoral deeds so that a more realistic chronicle of America may emerge. Here are recounted the mistakes, trickery and hatred which at times have directed America's destiny. While frankly debunking, I also attempt to shed new light on modern problems by tracing their development through U.S. history: racism, cruel exploitation of the Indian, violence and war, American imperialism and American poverty. The reader is no longer allowed the illusion that these are new problems but is confronted by the fact that America has always been possessed by these devils.

A well-known scholar, Carl Becker, once wrote an essay titled "What We Didn't Know Hurt Us a Lot." This title reflects something of the spirit, something of the intent, of this book. An ignorance of events which comprise United States history and of the existing critical interpretations of these events makes Americans susceptible to repeating the errors of the past. George Santayana's oft repeated maxim that "those who do not remember the past are condemned to repeat its mistakes" may unfortunately be applicable to most Americans who have been exposed to history mainly through the typical school curriculum. While there exists no "official" history of the United States as there does in Soviet Russia, nonetheless most of us are exposed to a "patriotic" interpretation of the U.S. history which is a Pollyanna misrepresentation of the American experience. Such accounts, stressing wars won, American moral superiority, and generally whitewashing American blunders and immorality are all too common even in college texts, and are the typical fare of high school and primary education. The history of poverty, racism and violence are ignored.

It is no wonder then that many of us fall into Santayana's hapless group of those doomed to repeat the mistakes of the past. *Reinterpreting American History* is offered as a remedy to such ignorance. Rarely mentioned facts are revealed such as the colonists' refusal of representation in Parliament so they could justify their failure to pay taxes with the hollow phrase, "No taxation without representation." Detailed accounts of certain events are reconstructed so that readers may understand the genesis of episodes which may be "whitewashed" in more typical renditions. For example, the course of events leading to America's declaration of war against Spain is described in order to reveal the immorality of this act after Spain had capitulated to America's every demand. In addition, new and critical interpretations of events such as the Revolution and World War II are offered to challenge the reader's time-worn misconceptions, acquaint him with alternative interpretations and to stimulate critical thinking. The reader is not allowed to remain comfortable with conventional images. Many histories view the conquest of America as a story of white men on the move from East to West Coast, bringing progress in their wake. I have written the truth—Americans land in Mexico, stealing huge tracts from the Indians, and finally destroying the native culture altogether.

This book is aimed at a broad readership. The book was written primarily for interested laymen, for those who, adult and young adult, want a fuller knowledge of the American heritage than the traditional education affords. Yet at the same time it is compact enough to allow a person to familiarize himself with revised interpretations of American history without delving into voluminous and difficult scholarly works. Hopefully lay readers will read this book simultaneously for both pleasure and information.

Ideally, *Reinterpreting American History* will also be used by college and high school teachers who use a "selected materials" approach or as supplementary reading to a more traditional textbook. It has become only too obvious that conventional survey courses of American history relying on traditional texts are frequently antiquated and obsolete. Racism, poverty and Vietnam have outmoded an uncritical review of the American story. Indeed, such a recitation is becoming impossible. Also, the traditional history text used in isolation has become obsolete for a second reason: students are sophisticated and probing as never before. They want to reflect on all sides of issues.

Reinterpretations of American history have been offered constantly in every changing form since the founding of the Republic (see Footnotes 1 and 2). As the world changes, the old interpretations of the past become antiquated and the emergence of new approaches is inevitable. George Bancroft, writing during the "Age of Jackson" in the 1930's, saw divine providence leading the nation toward greatness. As the "American frontier" came to an end in the 1890's, Frederick Jackson Turner attempted to explain the "American character" and the democratic nature of the society in terms of the frontier experience of the nation. Still later, historians in the optimistic years following World War II presumed to be telling the story *of the perfectability* of man in a democratic nation. Recent awareness of the present plight of minorities and civil rights calls for historical accounts which trace the often tragic course of ethnic minorities in America. The terrible possibility of a nuclear war leads to interpretations of past wars in terms of how they came about and how they might have been avoided. The past is always seen from the perspective of the important issues of the present.

I have included some character descriptions on the model of William E. Woodward's irreverent and delightful biography of George Washington. But most of the book presents in a more serious vein critical interpretations of the major political events of U.S. history. Such "revised" interpretations of individual historical events in scholarly works are becoming commonplace. I hope here to bring together revised interpretations of the entire American pageant, directed not at the scholars of history, but at the great majority whose knowledge has been shaped by traditional texts. The knowledgeable lay person will hopefully encounter many new facts and interpretations in these pages.

EDWARD F. DIENER

1. Kellum, David, *American History Through Conflicting Interpretations* (New York: Teachers College Press, 1969).

2. Wise, Gene, *American Historical Explanations* (Homewood, Illinois: Dorsey Press, 1973).

CHAPTER I

Prehistory and Colonization

Even schoolboys know Christopher Columbus didn't "discover" America, but many mistakenly believe this was the feat of a Norseman, Leif Ericson, in approximately 1000 A.D. Not true. Neither Leif nor other of his countrymen discovered America. It was inhabited thousands of years before by Asians, who first crossed from Siberia to the new land some 25,000 years ago. The Americas were the last continents to be settled, with the possible exception of Australia, because man first had to adapt culturally to the frozen Arctic before migration through Siberia was possible.

America's earliest inhabitants were hunters and gatherers, using simple stone and bone tools. The Asians migrated very slowly over North America and, by about 10,000 B.C., occupied most of what is now the United States. Occasional contact with the Orient continued, as proven by pottery patterns in later periods which reflect an Asian influence.

Natives of this age also were hunters; they lived in temporary shelters and migrated in small bands. Though they hunted deer and elk, there existed also more exotic prehistoric game—mastodons and mammoths, camels, and giant ground sloth. The last were bear-like creatures, up to twelve feet in height, their huge size typical of a period in which six-foot tall wolves and beavers the size of bears were common. Camels originated in North America, but became extinct domestically after some migrated to Asia; they were not seen in America again until reintroduced in zoos and used in the United States cavalry (an experiment which failed miserably). Horses were hunted, but not yet domesticated by America's Indians. Eventually, they grew extinct in America, only to be brought back in the 1500's by the conquistadors. Soon thereafter the Indians began to domesticate and ride them.

The desert Indians of the Southwest lived chiefly in caves and rock shelters, while natives of the East built wood and bark huts. A diversity of cultures existed between varying geographic areas, but, prior to the development of agriculture, there was little opportunity for rapid cultural progress. Farming existed in Mexico about 5,000 B.C., spreading to the Southwestern United States in about 2,000 B.C. By the time of Leif Ericson, small cities and nearly a million Indians abounded in the United States area. By 1492, well over 100 major tribes flourished in what we know today as America, each with distinct beliefs and ways of life, and possessing more than 50 basic language groups. The growth of agriculture generated rapid cultural change in the "new world," as had occurred in Europe. This evolution was brought to a halt by the arrival of the white settlers.

The history of the white man in America traditionally begins with Leif Ericson. The facts about the Norsemen are derived largely from sagas; thus, the details of their early discoveries are not certain. Leif's grandfather was apparently a pirate and plunderer who journeyed to Iceland after being deported from Norway. His son, Eric the Red, proved too wild even for desolate Iceland and was exiled to Greenland, where he founded a small settlement.

An early Norse mariner of unusual nautical skills, Bjarni Herjolfsson, attempted to reach this Greenland colony in 985 A.D. His craft was blown off course by gale winds, missed Greenland, and landed in Labrador, North America, antedating Leif's famed voyage by fifteen years. Bjarni barely explored the new continent, being anxious to return to Greenland at the first opportunity. When he did so he brought tales of the unknown continent with him, stirring the imagination of young Leif Ericson, son of Eric, founder of the Greenland colony. Leif eventually purchased Bjarni's ship and headed for Labrador about 1000 A.D., wintering in North America, where he did considerable exploring. Leif's crew built houses that first year in "Vinland," as they named it, and planned to erect a settlement there. The land derived the new name from its abundant wild grapes. Leif brought back a large cargo of timber to Greenland for use in housebuilding. His brother Thorwald then borrowed the ship and returned to North America for more extensive explorations. He fell in love with the new land and planned to build his home there, but a group of natives attacked his band and he was killed in the ensuing fight. His crew buried him at the site he had chosen for his new home. A small colony begun in Labrador about 1020 lasted three years.

Undoubtedly there were many later Norse expeditions to America; one well-documented one, in 1347, brought timber from Labrador to Iceland. Yet, although the Norse founded settlements in North America, the continuing hostility of the natives apparently drove them away. A map copied by a monk in 1430 from earlier Norse maps shows Labrador as "Vinland," supporting Bjarni's role in the early "discovery." Probably news of this new land spread to English sailors in Bristol, and perhaps even to Spain and Portugal. A Portuguese map of 1424 shows a land called Antilia occupying the position of present-day America. This may suggest either that earlier Mediterranean explorers had reached America or that Norse accounts of the New World had carried to the Iberian Peninsula. In either case, it appears that long before the time of Columbus vague knowledge of a new land to the West had spread throughout Europe. Nor did Columbus originate the idea that the world was round; this concept was widely accepted by Greek astronomers centuries earlier. Columbus did know that a great Florentine scholar, Toscanelli, had shown that the shortest route to the Orient was to travel west. Toscanelli knew from his studies that the world was round, and it was his theory which first brought this idea to Columbus.

Columbus's voyage was motivated not so much by scientific curiosity as by his self-seeking desire for fame and wealth. In the end he cheated and killed natives of the New World as he wandered between islands, but never succeeded in reaching the continent of North America, coming only as close as Cuba. Even so, Columbus ignored evidence that this was a land new to European explorers, persisting in his belief that it was the East Indies. The plants of the region were unknown in Asia and Europe; the natives neither spoke nor understood any of the languages of either continent. Yet Columbus held fast to his misguided notion and sent sailors searching through Cuba's jungles for the Khan's palace. Ultimately he died poor and angry, denying he had reached a "new land." Nor was his landing on islands near North America followed by a surge of European exploration and settlement, but, rather, over the next century, by a few scattered expeditions of freebooters dedicated to pillaging and searching for gold. Thus, even the claim that although Columbus did not discover America he spurred European settlement, is a myth.

Amerigo Vespucci visited America a few years after Columbus, and being an even better reporter than his predecessor, widely publicized his "find" throughout Europe upon his return. A German geographer read this account and labelled the new land after Vespucci on a map. The name "America" stuck.

A century intervened between the time of Columbus's voyages and the founding of the first English colonies in the "New World." England was only too glad to see many of her would-be colonists depart to a distant land. Just as good and upright men came to America, so did fanatics, fools, ne'er-do-wells, misguided adventurers and soldiers of fortune.

Sir Walter Raleigh sent a colony of 108 to Roanoke Island, North Carolina in the year 1585, after which the ships returned to England for supplies. These settlers struggled for a time against famine and the harassment of hostile natives, then gave up. When Sir Francis Drake landed on their island, they eagerly joined his return voyage to England. Several weeks after their departure, their ships returned to America with much-needed supplies and several new colonists, who elected to remain even after finding the island deserted. In 1587 a third expedition of English settlers reached Roanoke Island, under the leadership of John White, with the intent of moving the Roanoke colony to the mainland. But they too found the island deserted. There were no survivors from the second group of settlers to arrive at Roanoke. Alarmed at this, the colonists wished to launch their new colony on the mainland, but the ship's captain refused to take them any further, forcing them to remain on Roanoke Island. John White embarked for England to obtain more supplies, after leaving his daughter behind as a pledge to the colonists against his return. White's daughter gave birth to a baby girl, Virginia Dare, the first English child born in America. White's promised return was delayed for some four years. When he finally did arrive at Roanoke, no trace of the English settlers was to be found except the word "Croatoan" carved on a tree. It has been conjectured that these abandoned settlers went off to live with the Croatoan Indians, intermarried with them and were thus assimilated, one indication being the incidence of blue-eyed Indians in that area. The truth was never known, however, for, although White begged the ship's captain to sail to the neighboring Croatoan Island, the latter refused. White never saw his daughter again.

The first English colony to survive was Jamestown, founded in 1607 by the London Company. The ill-prepared band of colonists settled in a malarial swamp, failed to sow a single crop before winter, and succumbed to starvation and cold: over half of them died the first year. They were largely an ignorant, lazy and quarrelsome band. The London Company, instead of recruiting new colonists from among the farmers, who had hit upon bad times in England, filled its rolls mostly with criminals and idlers. The company was not motivated to establish a permanent farming community in the New World, but, rather, hoped for instant wealth from the discovery of gold. These Jamestown settlers had few usable skills and knew little of farming, being largely urban-born. Compounding their difficulties, soon after they landed at Jamestown they antagonized the native Indians, and thus were not only unable to trade with the Indians for food but were attacked repeatedly. The friendly Powhatan gave the settlers food which probably kept them from starvation that first winter, but failing to repay in kind, the settlers took whatever they desired by force. As a result the Indians soon became hostile and thereafter posed a constant threat.

Captain John Smith tried in vain to get the slothful band of settlers to work and plan. Many were too sick, and others simply refused. The London Company urged them to look for gold and many spent most of their time in a fruitless search, wasting prime farming months. A winter of grim starvation followed. Many more would have died had the population not already been greatly reduced by disease. Still, they resisted organization, with constant quarreling as the result. The settlers executed a member of their party on a minor allegation, and even cannibalism appeared.

The first English colony in Virginia was largely a disgrace and a failure. What ultimately saved it was the development of a valuable commodity, tobacco. Though the London Company was a financial failure, about a decade after its inception the colony at last began to flourish. Virginia itself prospered and grew through tobacco, although Jamestown never shared in this prosperity. It was burned in 1608, re-populated in 1610, and finally in 1676 was burned to the ground by a band of rebellious farmers protesting against the colonial government.

Plymouth, founded in 1620 by 100 settlers (only 35 of whom were Puritans), fared little better at first than had Jamestown. Although half the Plymouth settlers died the first winter, the group was better organized and generally more humane than their predecessors, and treated the Indians reasonably well. The Plymouth colony grew quickly as more new settlers arrived from England. The Puritans among them were religionists who wanted to "purify" the Anglican Church. When persecution of the Puritans in England intensified from 1630 to 1640, a great wave of them migrated to America. They were honest, hard working, and had a strong belief in education. (The colony founded Harvard in 1636.) Yet, they were intolerant and repressed those who dissented from their beliefs as harshly as they themselves had been repressed in England. Only Puritan males who owned property were allowed to vote. Since the Puritans were always in a minority in the colonies which they inhabited, they ruled as an undemocratic theocracy. Dissidents who professed religious ideas not wholly in accord with their own were banished from the colony. Puritan justice was extremely harsh, based on each judge's interpretation of the Old Testament. Puritanism fostered in its adherents rigidity, bigotry, and an abiding concern with sin. The Puritans were extremely pessimistic, believing all men were evil, "sinful" and "doomed." When the high standards of the early Puritans could not be maintained, laxity grew among the faithful. Eventually, the theocratic sway of its powerful religious ministers dwindled until, ultimately they lost political control.

America's cultural heritage is steeped in the Puritan ethic. The belief that man essentially is sinful and thereby doomed to hell, as well as the notion that material wealth reflects uprighteousness and God's favor, stimulated hard work and industriousness among the Puritans. This desire to achieve and prosper, like the willingness to work hard, have become inherent facets of the American value system.

After the founding of Plymouth, other Massachusetts settlements were started and soon other colonies emerged. Fortunately, in contrast to the Jamestown derelicts and the Puritan zealots, the bands of colonists included some farsighted settlers who were both practical and idealistic. Those who dissented against the Puritan beliefs launched other colonies, such as Rhode Island, which was founded by Roger Williams, who encouraged total religious freedom within his domain. In his relatively democratic Providence Plantation, Williams maintained strict separation of church and state. He purchased the site on which the settlement was founded from the Indians and believed that the settlers should maintain fair and friendly relations with them.

The Quakers also were persecuted by the Puritans, and in Massachusetts six were executed for refusing to change their beliefs to the Puritan dogma. The Quakers were pacifists whose religion contained no ritual. To them ministers were unnecessary, since they believed each member of the faith could achieve direct inner experience of God. Their leader, William Penn, directed the founding of what was to be an

19

outstanding colony. Rather than seizing the land, as had been the prevailing practice, Penn purchased title from the Indians. Under his leadership, the colony's government was fairly democratic, religious freedom prevailed, and the laws in force were just.

Another significant colony was that of Carolina, which was chartered by the King of England under a feudal system in which there were to be different ranks of nobility analogous to dukes, earls, and so on. This settlement exemplified the only attempt by the Crown to introduce its system of nobility into the colonies. Though large grants of land were made, the feudal manors never prospered, chiefly because no vassals could be recruited. This was due to the fact that any white settler could acquire land of his own, and thus none were willing to work as peasants for a feudal lord. Carolina soon developed a system much like that of other colonies and attained moderate prosperity.

The colony of Georgia was founded by James Oglethorpe and an associated group of philanthropists for the noble purpose of creating a sanctuary for English religious dissenters, as well as indigent debtors, who often were jailed in England. The Crown and Parliament granted a charter to the new colony (and the generous sum of 10-million pounds), motivated mainly by the desire to create a buffer between the Indians and Spaniards in Florida and the other English colonies to the North. Religious dissenters and the poor thereby would bear the brunt of attacks from the Spaniards and from the hostile Southern Indians. The Georgia colony, though successful, failed notably as a social experiment. Its early ban on slaves was soon rescinded and laws limiting land holdings to fifty acres per family were easily circumvented. The Georgia colonists refused to live the strict, disciplined life dictated by Oglethorpe, and his supporters soon withdrew their trusteeship, sorely disappointed in the moral laxity of the settlers. Nonetheless, the King willingly granted them a royal charter, for although rum was flowing freely in Georgia, its settlers were willing to do battle with England's foes to the south. It doubtless suited the Crown better to have in Georgia rough and ready rebels rather than reformed debtors mindful only of the laws set forth by Oglethorpe.

From the very onset of colonization in America, mistreatment of the native Indians was commonplace. In the two centuries preceding the Revolution barely a tribe was exempt from the white man's treachery. One instance is that of colonist William Kieft, appointed governor of New Netherlands (New York) in 1638. Kieft initiated his relations with the neighboring Algonquian tribes by levying a tax on them for the stated purpose of protecting them from the fierce Iroquois to the north, who did, in fact, soon attack the Algonquians. However, Kieft didn't raise a hand to help the Algonquians whom he had contracted to protect.

On one occasion an Algonquian Indian woman was murdered by a Dutch settler, who charged her with stealing his peaches. When an Indian relative avenged her death by killing the Dutch farmer, Kieft demanded the tribe deliver him over for punishment. The tribe refused. Kieft answered the Indian denial by dispatching an expedition against the Indians. An eyewitness account tells of the grim atrocity:

> When it was day the soldiers returned to the fort, having massacred or murdered eighty Indians, and considering that they had done a deed of Roman valour, in murdering so many in their sleep, where infants were torn from their mothers' breasts and the pieces thrown in the fire and in the water, and other sucklings were bound to small boards and then cut, struck, and pierced, and miserably massacred in a manner to move a heart of stone. Some were thrown into the river, and when the fathers and mothers endeavored to save them, the soldiers would not let them come on land but made both parents and children drown, children from five to six years of age, and also some decrepit persons. . . .

Ben Franklin described a similar massacre about a century later in 1764 with the sole difference that no Indian action had provoked it. The crime was perpetrated against the Conestoga Indians. This tribe had always maintained extremely friendly relations with the Pennsylvania settlers, sending messages of greeting to each new governor and giving much of their time and assistance to the white settlements. The tribe was very small, a total of only twenty, on the night in 1724 when 57 whites surrounded its village and killed six of its people. Franklin noted the whites were pleased with their success, but angered that fourteen Indians had escaped their rightful fate. Nonetheless, they tracked the remaining Indians, located them in a neighboring white settlement, and massacred them in a manner similar to the killings under Kieft in New Netherlands. The murderers then marched toward Philadelphia, the capital, to demand help in fighting neighboring Indian tribes, announcing they had murdered the innocent Conestoga in protest against governmental apathy to Indian attacks. That the Conestoga were a wholly peaceful tribe and uninvolved in the alleged attacks had not mattered. Yet Ben Franklin, who several years later wrote condemningly of these murders, was so fearful this band of rampant white killers would attack Philadelphia that he sought to dissuade them from doing so by promising a bounty on Indian scalps!

Thus, even Franklin, usually a fair man, jeopardized Indian lives to pacify a group of murderers. This aggression toward the natives which had become a tradition in the evolving United States, continued until the Indians were a totally devastated people. Kieft once recommended that the Indians "should by force of arms be utterly destroyed and exterminated." This was the first official statement of the unwritten policy of white colonial leaders and militarists during the inception of the American nation. It was to be the program of the white peoples of the United States, if not also of their government. Even in this early period of the nation's history white expansion was always at the expense of the Indian.

Some of the primitive customs and events of America's white colonies merit discussion. Among these are the witchcraft trials, crime in the cities, and the farmer's uprisings. The Salem witchcraft trials of 1692, unfortunate though they were, are often misunderstood and unjustly condemned. The grim events stemmed from accusations of witchcraft made by some teenage girls in Salem. Many people thereafter were tried as witches, and 19 actually executed. One such sentence was carried out by placing the condemned man between large boards, then piling heavy boulders atop the upper plank until he was crushed.

Yet several misconceptions have grown up around these trials. The contention that no acts of witchcraft occurred and that witchcraft did not work are both false. Cotton Mather, a Puritan cleric who had written a book on witchcraft, *Memorable Providences Relating to Witchcraft and Possessions*, presided at the Salem trials and therefore reaps much of the blame for the proceedings. Mather actually was a fair judge who weighed the merits of each case individually and condemned no one without what seemed to him sound and indisputable evidence.

It is mistaken to believe that no witchcraft was practiced and that public hysteria resulted solely from overstimulated imaginations. Witches, who regarded themselves as agents of Satan, lived at the time in both England and America and actively practiced their avocation. All those executed for witchcraft certainly were not witches, but it is virtually as certain that some of them practiced witchcraft. The great error of generations thereafter was to assume that witches did not exist. For, although none possessed supernatural powers nor flew on broomsticks, there were persons who believed themselves to be witches and accordingly performed the most bizarre acts.

Even more startling to modern man is the fact that spells cast by witches were effective. Scientists recently have affirmed that voodoo is quite effective in killing those who believe in or fear it. Indeed, psychologists have studied the practice of "boning" among aborigines in Australia, in which the witch doctor points a bone at a subject and directs an appropriate curse. Invariably the subject dies in comatose shock within several days. This practice takes a similar toll on outsiders only when they believe in its efficacy. The Salem witchcraft practitioners undoubtedly affected their victims through this same psychological process, so that believers in the occult who were cursed either died or were afflicted with psychosomatic paralysis or disability. Doubtless the witch's curse induced real and severe suffering to the vulnerable. Thus, those who brought the accused witches to trial justly were trying them for criminal acts, since their incantations had caused real harm to others. This harm was no less criminal because it was inflicted psychologically, rather than physically, for the anguish and suffering of the victims were no less real. Once the widespread popular belief in witchcraft diminished, so did its power to afflict, and thus the need for trials and punishment of its practitioners.

America's history texts affirm that crime in the cities is not a new problem—colonial America had a severe crime rate and little means of controlling it. Mugging and rape were such frequent occurrences in larger cities, such as Philadelphia and New York, that people could not travel alone in the streets at night. Gangs of thugs roamed the cities, burglarizing and looting. Mobs occasionally rioted in Boston and other large cities. Rioting is an integral facet of America's history, plaguing virtually every era to this day. Another heinous crime, infanticide, was also common. Less serious offenses that were prevalent included gambling, cockfighting, and the cruel sport of baiting bears and bulls with fierce dogs. Though some more serious crimes were punishable by death, this apparently had little deterrent value. Prostitution was also common in the colonies.

Though colonial America was essentially rural, with some ninety-five percent of the population living in the country, agricultural areas often had little political power. The fact that a small minority of Eastern city-dwellers maintained political control fomented several rural uprisings in the colonial years. One occurred in 1676, when a band of Virginia farmers were doubly agitated by the levying of a poll tax and the toll exacted by Indian attacks. Led by Nathaniel Bacon, the small army of farmers attacked and killed some peaceful local Indians, then stormed and burned their capital, Jamestown. They ultimately were subdued, and several tried and executed. A similar rebellion was that of the "Paxton Boys" in 1763, previously mentioned in conjunction with the murder of the Conestoga

Indians. A third uprising occurred in North Carolina in 1771, fomented by frontiersmen known as the "Regulators." After a bloody battle, government troops subdued the rebels and tried and hanged their leaders. Despite these hangings, two notable aspects of most such rebellions were that the participants largely went unpunished, and often successfully achieved their purpose. This gentling of rioters and rebels alike served only to increase and intensify future outbursts. As a result, riots became more and more a part of the American way of life.

Following the early colonization of America, the first really significant historic event was the French and Indian War. War is a phenomenon deeply rooted in the American saga and this was the first large conflict in which the colonists fought. America gained its first real glimpse of George Washington, and even more importantly, the war indirectly triggered the Revolution that was to break out some twenty years later.

America's first national hero, George Washington, was at the time of the French and Indian War a gangling youth of 21 who was so inarticulate he could barely make himself understood. The conflict provided George with an opportunity to prove his incompetence as a military leader. The French and English territories, once separated by wilderness, had expanded outward over the years until the French erected a series of forts on land which the English claimed to be their territory. A colonial governor dispatched Washington to French headquarters to warn them they were on English soil and must relinquish it immediately. The French commandant greeted this as a joke, laughed heartily, and sent Washington packing back to Virginia.

Governor Dinwiddie then dispatched Washington with 150 troops back to the French fort to rout the enemy. The initial appraisal of the French officer who had treated Washington with such disdain soon proved to be well-founded. The French hopelessly outnumbered Washington's forces, but when they marched against him he chose to stand ground and fight, rather than order a strategic retreat. He further compounded the gravity of his error by choosing the worst possible terrain on which to make a stand. Thus, he established "Fort Necessity" not in a high spot, which would have been easier to defend, but in an open marsh, totally surrounded by timbered slopes. It didn't require the mind of a military strategist to foresee the result. The French used the trees for cover while enjoying a clear lead on Washington's fully-exposed forces. To his credit, Washington quickly surrendered. However, he then committed a further blunder. He was duped into signing an official confession stating that he had assassinated a French officer. This highly incriminating admission was completely untrue.

After disarming Washington and his men, the French permitted them to march back to the English colonies. Yet, amazingly, on his return to Virginia Washington was greeted as a hero. Despite this, Governor Dinwiddie, reviewing his performance against the French more realistically than had most of the colonists, demoted him in rank for his poor handling of the assignment. The demotion, though deserved, caused Washington to resent Dinwiddie and the English government which he represented. It was undoubtedly a decisive factor in his opting to fight against the British during the Revolution.

A year after Washington's Fort Necessity fiasco, he returned with a large British army to confront the French. This time, however, Washington was not in charge, but served under a prominent British officer, General Edward Braddock. Washington was now a volunteer, serving without pay or rank. Though humiliated by his demotion, he nevertheless was eager to prove himself. In the confrontation the British Army was completely decimated, some 1400 British being killed, including the courageous Braddock. Washington took charge of the 500 survivors and took the most expedient course: he led a retreat.

Upon his return to Virginia, Washington complained of the cowardice of the British soldiers in contrast to the bravery of the colonists. Yet he was later unable to rally a viable colonial force when the French seized the offensive and attacked the colonies. The colonists were not interested in becoming soldiers. Even among those in the army, the desertion rate was high. They were willing to fight only if their own homes were threatened and otherwise would not leave their immediate territory. They had little concern for the fate of neighboring colonies or those outside their area. Once any imminent threat had subsided, the major part of the defense for the 13 colonies was provided by the British, with little help from the colonists. Though attempts were made to muster a local militia they failed, and the meager force quickly disbanded.

The famed British General, James Wolfe, had little more than contempt for the colonial soldiers, who, said some of his officers, were "broken innkeepers, horse jockeys and Indian traders." Washington, at odds with the English military, attempted to uphold the honor of the colonial army, but could not rouse the colonists to enlist or serve. When he sought to organize a defense for Winchester, Virginia in 1757, he could muster only 40 men. As a result, the French attacked the town at will, as well as the entire Shenandoah alley.

How Washington continued as an officer is difficult to understand. When he was not losing battles or failing in his efforts to muster volunteers, he was submerged either in melancholic depression or dysentery (which kept him bedridden for many months during the war). America had created a national hero, albeit one whose achievements were modest. Though historic records may hint at Washington's overriding incompetence, America in that day had no folk heroes, and apparently he was the best it could choose.

The real significance of the French and Indian War was that it substantially triggered the American Revolution two decades later. It is important to realize the role of the French and Indian War in the events which were to follow in the next twenty years. The British expended vast sums of money fighting the French. They viewed this as an expenditure in defense of the colonies. Though willing to bear the staggering costs of the war, England believed the colonies should contribute to the costs of their defense thereafter, and thus levied duties and taxes accordingly. The colonists, conversely, seemed happy to have the British defending their settlements and fighting in defense of their territory, but continually resisted all requests to help support the continuing costs of defense. A second result of the war which eventually would lead to Revolution was that now, with the menacing French repelled, the colonists felt less in need of their mother country's protection against invaders. England had thus spent British lives and millions defending the colonists, who quickly forgot the gift and wanted the fruits of victory for themselves. They were unwilling to contribute to England's defense of their new land, but, at the same time, felt secure and wanted to be free from any of the obligations inherent in the operation of a stable government.

CHAPTER II

The American Rebellion

The American Revolution is perhaps the most glorified event in national history, one all Americans allegedly reflect upon with great pride and quickened heartbeats. Is America's birth held sacred to link it with political divinity? Surely nothing bolsters nationalistic vanity more than notions of a birthright free of sin. Such motivation underlies the enshrinement of the American Revolution: the myth that America was forged in the quest for goodness and purity. But we know that myths are not truth.

In truth America was a bastard, an illegitimate offspring conceived in sin, born in violence, and suckled on the pap of protest. Our forefathers begat America after refusing to act responsibly as British subjects. The birth-pangs were wanton destruction and death. But a nation was born, however ignominiously.

The myth which should be exploded first, because it is the most pernicious, is that the colonies were ruled harshly, even despotically, by the British. Not true. American colonists were asked to contribute through taxes a small portion of the revenue needed to administer colonial government and defense. These taxes were minimal, compared to those being levied in England. But the colonists balked. Thus colonial assemblies were repeatedly consulted and alternate proposals to the tax requested. Neither proposals nor taxes were forthcoming. The colonists were then offered representation in Parliament, from which laws and tax levies emanated for the entire empire. This was rejected flatly.

The real cause of the Revolution? The colonists' careful avoidance of every responsibility that stable, effective government requires of its citizens. They refused to elect representatives to work for change through existing institutions; they refused to support the government through equitable taxes; and they shamelessly breached the laws, which agitated British lawmakers and made British retaliation inevitable.

The French and Indian War set the stage in America for the events of the next half-century. This war was of monumental import to the development of the embryo nation. It triggered the American Revolution, but more importantly, its outcome determined which civilization, which political institutions and which cultural patterns would dominate the west, and eventually, the entire North American continent. The English inheritance of the American mainland and most of Canada stemmed from the British victory in 1763. Only against the background of this great war can the events leading to the American Revolution be fully understood.

In 1754 the French threatened the peace and territorial claims of British Americans. The latter petitioned Parliament for aid. British troops were dispatched to intervene on their behalf. A war was soon ignited which ultimately was won by the British. It is essential to understand that England engaged in this war chiefly in defense of her colonies.

For England the war meant enormous costs. Vast sums had to be borrowed to cover them. While the English were heavily assessed, the American colonists paid no taxes, though England had spent great sums administering colonial government and defenses. After the war the costs of maintaining garrisons in the West and Canada necessary to the peace and defense of the area increased Britain's costs still further. Thus Britain looked to the American colonists for aid. It seemed fitting they should contribute a third of the revenues needed for maintaining their own defense and administration.

In retrospect the British offer seems generous, since British garrisons directly defending the colonies were of no advantage to the English tax payers 3,000 miles away. Nor, during the French and Indian war, were the American colonists asked to contribute to any of the costs of defending their territory. They were asked only to pay one-third of the continuing expenses for defense. Without British aid the colonists would have had to support their military wholly at their own expense, and a very inadequate military at that. Nor could they rely on the world's greatest navy to protect them against the threats of foreign powers. But the colonists continued to balk at proposed taxation.

The French and Indian War also proved an important antecedent to the Revolution in another way. The treasonous trading by colonial merchants with the enemy during wartime was irksome to the British. This factor among others led England to view the colonists as disloyal ingrates, many of whom were criminals and cutthroats. Another cause of the Revolution stemming from the earlier war was the relative security of the American continent from French threats, which led the colonists to feel aggressively self-sufficient.

The final spark was struck by Parliament when it established the Proclamation Line across the Appalachians in 1763. White settlements, it declared, were not to advance west of this line. In compensation to the colonists for this loss of territory Parliament created three new colonies, Quebec, East Florida, and West Florida. This action stirred strong colonial resentment against Imperial rule that was to be a prelude to the events of the future. The colonists protested the Proclamation Line, claiming the British were trying to stifle colonial expansion. In actuality the Line had been established as a temporary expedient to help achieve peace among the Indians and fulfill promises made to them during the French and Indian War.

The greed of colonial land speculators and frontiersmen soon spawned their open violations of the line. Once again the British witnessed the colonists' flagrant violations of British law. Parliament at last acquiesced to American protests against the Line and withdrew it several years later, even though the English had negotiated treaties with the Indians for much of the land the colonists desired. In withdrawing the line the British demonstrated their desire to treat the colonies fairly, but also inadvertently indicated that transgressions against

British law would not only not be punished, but might actually be rewarded.

Import duties, collectively called the Sugar Act, were the vehicle by which the British first attempted to collect revenue from the colonists to cover the costs of war and continuing defense. They were also instituted as a means of controlling trade. Many colonial shippers openly violated trade laws when it was profitable and easy to do so, smuggling goods or bribing port officials in order to evade tariffs or bypass trade restrictions. Thus measures were enacted by Parliament to enforce the new mercantile levies.

American opposition to the Sugar Act was swift and vigorous. As a result they were soon repealed. Again, the British had made every effort to be fair, but this last concession only reinforced the colonists' naive belief that the Crown would allow them anything they wished if they protested loudly enough. Some even began claiming Parliament had no right to legislate for the colonies. The British petitioned colonial assemblies to submit alternate ideas on how the needed revenue from the colonists might be collected.

Under one plan proposed by the British, each colony would have been assessed a given sum with its assembly free to raise the amount through whatever means it deemed appropriate. This plan was considered by some assemblies, but rejected. Despite England's request, no suggestions were tendered by the colonies.

After the Sugar Act was repealed the Stamp Act was effected which, in another effort to collect the needed revenue, levied a tax upon all printed matter. Though the act had been opposed by the colonists prior to its passage, the British had actually believed they would ultimately accept it. After all, it was fair and obvious benefit to the colonies, since it provided revenue for their defense. But the colonists refused to pay the new tax. Instead they rioted and destroyed government property. The "Liberty Boys" reacted violently, burning government records along with the hated stamps and looting the homes of British officials. The law proved impossible to enforce and was repealed the following year.

The cry "No taxation without representation!" so well publicized in American history texts, was a noble-sounding slogan behind which thousands evaded taxes. Parliament had passed many laws regulating the colonies, including tax levies, but not discriminatingly; the colonies were represented in Parliament in the same way most English subjects were, by "virtual," rather than direct, representation. This term delineated it as the duty of every member of Parliament to act in the interests of the entire empire and its people, both the colonists and those in England. Only three percent of all English subjects at the time were qualified to vote. Thus many counties in England elected no representatives, but were accorded virtual representation instead. Even more telling is the fact that colonial assemblies rejected representation when that possibility was informally proposed by the Prime Minister. Virginia and South Carolina, as well as other colonies, voiced open objection to the prospect of occupying seats in Parliament, and the idea was subsequently tabled by the ministry, which acknowledged correctly that the colonies had no interest in such representation. The Massachusetts Assembly lay open the heart of the matter, saying that taxes without representation were preferable to taxes with it. Their statement makes clear they declined representation in order to later use the absence of colonial seats in Parliament as an excuse for their refusal to pay taxes. Thus the colonists were responsible for lack of representation, not the British. Nonetheless the colonials would have balked at paying taxes even if local assemblies had levied them, since they were generally unwilling to pay the costs of government, defense, or any other British services aiding their survival.

The riots staged by the colonists against the Stamp Act alarmed Parliament, which already was agitated by colonial defiance of virtually every British law. When the British enacted other tariffs, notably the Townshend Acts, they stirred even greater opposition from the colonies. In addition, colonial agitators such as Samuel Adams were unsettling the Crown with pronouncements that Parliament had no right to ratify any law governing the American colonies. England's fear of colonial anarchy combined with increased determination to enforce law in the colonies prompted stronger governmental action than ever. After the Stamp Act riots, the British government increased its military forces in the colonies.

Yet, the British continued their errant benevolence; in 1770, they repealed the Townshend Acts. Like spoiled children the colonists again had gotten their way through noisy tantrums of violence and lawlessness.

The repeal of the Townshend Acts restored colonial calm until 1772, when rampant lawlessness in the colonies prodded the Crown to adopt sterner measures. A British patrol boat, Gaspee, had run aground while pursuing a colonial smuggler. That night colonists stormed the boat, wounded the captain, and set the vessel ablaze. When attempts were made to bring the pirates to justice no one would testify against them. It was the colonists' refusal to cooperate in bringing the case to justice, more than the lawless act itself, which infuriated the British. The following year occasioned the Boston Tea Party, another criminal offense, which historians over the years have glossed over as one of America's great, heroic events. Again, it was not the crime alone which angered the Crown, but realization that the guilty colonists would never be brought to justice.

England was now more convinced than ever that the colonies championed lawlessness and would neither cooperate with nor contribute to British colonial government. The Crown decided to exert its control and ratified the so-called "Coercive Acts" to discipline Massachusetts for its part in the Tea Party.

A mistaken belief prevails that the English mercantile laws, which controlled trade within the British Empire as well as with foreign nations, were written solely to benefit the British motherland. In fact these laws were designed to further the entire empire by fostering different specialization in different areas, thereby increasing efficiency. At the same time, foreign products were taxed so that those within the empire would be encouraged to buy goods produced therein. For example, Virginia tobacco-growers benefited greatly from mercantile laws which gave that colony a monopoly over the product, forbidding its growth in Ireland and England. These laws stimulated

34

Virginia's tobacco industry, benefitting both Mother Country and the colonies. The import restrictions and duties comprising the mercantile laws aimed at helping both England and her colonies, and were hardly measures of colonial oppression.

The eve of Revolution came quickly. The first shots were fired at Lexington and Concord in 1775, the year before the colonies declared themselves independent.

The Loyalists, or Tories, were actually the patriots of the Revolution. They knew some complaints against the Crown were justified, yet they chose to work peacefully for change. They retained faith in the democratic institutions which had helped make England great, faith that grievances could be resolved through the democratic process. It often has been said that George Washington himself would have been a Loyalist had he obtained a promotion after Braddock's defeat in the French and Indian War. Washington was a bonded aristocrat who turned against the English when they failed to give him a royal commission after he led the retreat of Braddock's troops. The Loyalists, many of whom were doctors, lawyers, teachers, and others on the professional level, did not see a permanent break with England as the sole solution to the problems of the colonies.

In contrast to the Loyalists were the agitators, such as Samuel Adams and Patrick Henry, often motivated more by self-gain rather than love of freedom, who continually incited protests against the Mother Country. In times of calm, when non-violent resolution of conflicts seemed imminent, the agitators aggressively revived old issues and aroused new ire through their oratory and propaganda. These incendiaries cared little for peaceful resolution of old disputes, desiring revolution and nothing less in the hope their personal fortunes would soar with the coming of home rule to the colonies under their stewardship. Thus, while the Loyalists worked for a peaceful solution, Samuel Adams and his cohorts fanned the fires of conflict. The revolution was not a sudden event, but the outgrowth of a decade of rioting and upheaval incited by radicals that grew eventually into a full-scale rebellion, supported by approximately one-third of America's colonists.

35

America's war for independence was not a "revolution" in the real meaning of the word. As historian Daniel Boorstin observed:

> The Revolution itself . . . had been a kind of affirmation of faith in British institutions. In the greater part, the institutional life of the community of the Revolution thus required no basic change . . . it also helps to account for the value which we still attach to our inheritance from the British constitution: trial by jury, due process of law, representation before taxation, habeas corpus, freedom from attainder, independence of the judiciary, and the rights of free speech, free petition, and free assembly, as well as our narrow definition of treason. . . .

The war did not mean the overthrow of social institutions nor the adoption of a new philosophy. Americans often mistakenly attribute to the Revolution their heritage of personal freedoms and democracy, but these legacies were actually those of the mother country.

Though America bore a major part of the responsibility for the Revolution, ultimately, she triumphed. But this victory was not easily attained. More than once during the war miscarriage threatened. Disunity riddled the colonies; only a third were rebels at the outset of the war, another third, uncommitted, and the remainder, loyal to England. Many soldiers would fight only if their own region were threatened; their loyalty was solely to their area. Other deficits hampered the young nation's course, not the least of which was George Washington. As a general, his command was often disappointing. While at times he functioned commendably, his overall performance as a military chief was mediocre. French General Conway, serving under the Americans, said that God must have decided beforehand in favor of the Americans, or else they surely would have been defeated under Washington's command. As we examine the course of the war, the accuracy of this evaluation becomes apparent.

The initial appointment of Washington as Commander-in-Chief was questionable since his military record was unexceptional. Although he had "captured" Fort Duquesne in the French and Indian War, this had been no noteworthy feat since the fort had been abandoned at the time. Washington denied he desired the position, though he was the only statesman to wear military dress to daily Congressional Sessions. Seated there in a resplendent officer's uniform, replete with braid and brass, the big fellow vehemently denied he had any designs on the top rank. Washington feigned reluctance and humility to gain it, a psychological tactic he would use successfully again to gain the Presidency. He was named Commander-in-Chief as the result of a sectional compromise. Powerful Virginia agreed to support New England's armies only if her native son could lead them. Washington accepted, adding that he was "not fit" for the job.

He had not yet assumed command when the famous Battle of Bunker Hill was fought in 1775. War had begun; there was no turning back now. Americans were heartened to discover they could fight as well as the British, who won the battle but suffered heavy casualties. Washington stated immodestly that he would win the war "in several months." After he fortified a position overlooking Boston the British withdrew rather than risk another bloody battle for a victory of questionable strategic value.

The next large encounters were those in New York. At this early stage Washington's tactical bungling easily could have forfeited the Revolution. In the first encounter at Long Island they were outflanked, soundly defeated, and their commander almost captured. Washington's troops performed badly, running "almost by whole regiments." Only Britain's ambivalence, its uncertainty whether to crush the colonists or sue for peace with them, saved the American Army. If Howe, the British general, had swept boldly down on the colonists the Revolution would have been over. But he was reluctant and Washington was saved, by no efforts of his own, to fight another day.

That day came quickly, in the Battle of Manhattan, and again the rebels proved no match for the English. Terrified colonists fled the battlefield despite Washington's threats to shoot them. Washington, historians claim, "greatly inspired" his troops; yet he stood at Harlem Heights, shouting, while all about him his troops fled. Close to entire regiments had fled at Long Island, and desertion was to plague the harried general throughout the war. The "spirit" Washington allegedly instilled in his troops was nowhere reflected in their behavior. Whereas Napoleon, the greatest military leader since Alexander had perceived the advantages of motivating his troops with such rewards as medals, promotions and praise, Washington used a wholly negative approach—criticism, flogging, and execution. His feelings for his men are reflected in his view of them as "exceeding and dirty nasty people."

Yet Washington's ability to inspire his troops was notable compared to his strategic skills. He posted his army on Manhattan Island, a most vulnerable locale considering British naval strength. While common sense dictated a quick retreat to the North he stayed put. When, after his defeat at Harlem Heights, Washington finally retreated to comparatively safe New Jersey, he left a large contingent at Manhattan. The folly of leaving the troops behind was obvious; they soon were captured by Howe. In the course of a few months' fighting, Washington's army had been reduced by deaths, capture, and desertion to barely 3,000 men.

Thereafter, he won the Battles of Trenton and Princeton, neither of them strategically important. Historians often hail these as "big" victories because American spirits had been at low ebb in the wake of the New York rout, and even these insignificant victories renewed colonial hopes. The Battle of Trenton was highly irregular in that Washington attacked the morning after Christmas Day, considered by militarists of that time as an armistice period. Some branded the attack "immoral."

The following year witnessed an important colonial victory, but not under Washington's leadership. Benedict Arnold, Philip Schuyler, and Horatio Gates forced Burgoyne's surrender at Saratoga, a major triumph since it led the French to agree to alliance with America. In the next battle—Brandywine—Washington was soundly defeated, with Howe using precisely the same tactics that had routed the Americans at Long Island. Washington had not learned his lesson very well.

Next Howe feinted Washington out of position and marched into the nation's capital, Philadelphia, unopposed. Congress fled to New York. More blunders by Washington cost the next battle at Germantown. While the battle loomed hopefully for the American forces at the outset, Washington divided his troops into two sections. As one group fought gallantly, he wasted the others by using them to lay siege to a house. The absence of needed reinforcements cost the forward group a possible victory. Again, Washington's inexperience as a tactician lost the battle and countless American lives.

The grueling winter at Valley Forge was to follow. History texts fail to note that the starvation among the ranks that winter took place in the heart of a rich agricultural region. Then why such hunger? The local farmers had sold their stores of grain and livestock to the British, who had offered a higher price. The famine at Valley Forge resulted from American greed, and those who suffered and died that winter did so at the hands of their American countrymen. Many deserted Washington that grim season to return home; others defected to the British Army. Congress had been noticeably disappointed with Washington's military performance to date. Some, such as Samuel Adams, spoke of replacing him, but a movement to do so was not successful.

After Valley Forge Washington's troops attacked the rear flank of the British Army as it moved from Philadelphia to New York. This battle at Monmouth (1778), if better managed, could have netted a decisive American victory, rather than the standoff it produced. The next winter at Morristown witnessed much of the suffering of the year before, with some of Washington's troops rising in mutiny against him. Two more attempts at mutiny occurred and twelve American soldiers were executed.

In 1780 a large complement of French Army troops under General Rochambeau landed in Rhode Island. They had come to aid Washington's campaign but were largely ignored. Not only did the American Commander treat the needed French reinforcements coolly, but he let them waste away idly for the better part of a year. They reacted with growing bitterness toward the Americans.

Historians characteristically have accorded sole credit to Washington for the victory at Yorktown, the last major engagement of the war. Perhaps charitably, since this was the only significant major victory achieved under his command. Yet credit for his success was largely due the French. While Washington had favored attacking New York, the perils and pitfalls of that plan were ominous. Rochambeau favored a strike against Cornwallis in Virginia, and this plan, vastly superior to Washington's, was chosen. In addition, the French had to finance Washington's army in this campaign since the American treasury was bare.

The battle ensued and Cornwallis at last was surrounded at Yorktown. His escape by sea was blocked by the French fleet. Though half the allied troops which defeated Cornwallis were French regulars and many of the American militiamen were undependable novices, the victory was credited to Washington. It belonged largely to the French. After Yorktown, the fighting subsided and there was little of it for nearly two years. Then, in 1783, the final treaty with Britain was ratified by Congress.

It had not been God or George Washington who had wrought the American triumph, but the French, Dutch, and Spanish, who had been fighting England concurrently with the Revolution. At the time, England was engaged on battle fronts scattered over four continents, and her forces, thus distended, were not faring well. When she granted America independence, it was because she wanted to launch all her forces against her chief enemy, France. Though America had not humbled the great British Empire, she fortuitously had chosen a time when England was vulnerable and world events made the Revolution possible.

From the conflict Washington emerged the unlikeliest of military heroes, a cold aristocrat, wealthy, out of touch with the common man. His battlefield blunder had not earned him the reputation of a brilliant general. Undeniably he had been courageous in battle, but the war had been won less because of, than in spite of, his strategies. But the nation was new and young and needed heroes.

Though the causes justifying the Revolution were weak at best and the war effort often badly executed, a new nation had emerged, and with it, national heroes. Yet it should be remembered that "heroes" are men and have their weaknesses. Thomas Jefferson, for example, wrote eloquently of the equality of all men in the Declaration of Independence, yet manifested prejudice against Negroes. Some of his writings on blacks would be regarded as racial today. Yet he seemed untroubled about the inconsistency of these personal views with his lofty pronouncements in the Declaration. Jefferson was not one to let contradictions bother him. Despite his condemnation of blacks, he maintained a Negro mistress, Sally Hemmings, for some twenty years, with four illegitimate children resulting. Another prominent paradox was that heroic horseman, Paul Revere, who was accused of cowardice and disobedience while serving as a commissioned officer during the Revolution. He lost his reputation in a battle in which the Americans performed so badly that it became a scandal throughout the colonies. John Hancock, too, and other exalted statesmen amassed personal fortunes during the Revolution, often misusing their positions of public trust to make money. The Revolution treated Hancock well in another way; he was scheduled to be tried for smuggling on the very day the conflict began. He not only escaped trial but accumulated a fortune.

Ben Franklin pursued his own noted sexual dalliance with flair and gusto. For Franklin, sex was not merely a drive; it was a devotion. Though Washington, sterile from childhood, often is called the "Father of His Country," Franklin who spawned his love without discrimination of creed, color, or class, fathered children in every sector of colonial society, and thus, more accurately deserves this distinction. "Low and lewd women" as well as the very rich, married or unmarried— Franklin greeted them all with open arms. Nor was he adverse to age, which may explain his great amatory success. Though Franklin enjoyed the company of beautiful young ladies, he enumerated the advantages of the older ones: they had experience, couldn't become pregnant, and were so very grateful afterward. The pronouncement was to characterize Franklin's tireless quest for fleshly pleasures throughout most of his eighty-four years.

Perhaps the greatest misnomer accorded George Washington was his "honesty." Nothing could be less true. In surveying land for the Crown, he managed to steal 30,000 acres for himself. When a bill enacted in England threatened to deprive George of his stolen property, he asked Ben Franklin to "fix it" up (that is, bribe officials in London.) In truth, Washington valued luxury far more than honesty. To live luxuriously, even royally, he was willing to sacrifice anything, including his own integrity and his troops. If his greatest misdeeds did not occur during the American Revolution, they were at least the most well-documented. As Commander-in-Chief, he was offered by Congress $500 per month salary (equivalent to $10,000 today at the inflation-conversion rate of 20-1.) Washington pointedly declined the generous salary, since he was wealthy already, and asked only for expenses. Congress was gratified at this reasonable request. Yet after eight years as Commander-in-Chief, his expenses totaled $450,000! This was approximately ten times the proposed salary he would have received for that period, and the equivalent of some $10,000,000 dollars today. Washington annually spent over what would be $1,000,000 today on wholly personal expenses. And Congress paid the bill.

It is known that Washington lived royally at government expense, setting a precedent for future Presidential spending. But what of the hardships endured by the American Army during the Revolution—did they not also afflict General Washington? Ironically, no! While the starving troops ate roots, bark, and even rawhide remnants of boots, Washington dined well at lavish feasts and drank heartily of Madeira wine. Lacking shelter and supplies, the half-naked troops froze in deep snows through one of the bitterest winters in New England history. Washington, in his great-coat and grand regalia, had shelter, warmth, and a full complement of manor comforts.

But Washington did not feel any guilt. His well-itemized expenses were quite "legitimate": two new horses a year, averaging $1,500 each, $500 to $900 per month for spirits, $28,000 for Martha's visits to his winter quarters. When one realizes dollars then were worth many times their value today, Washington's spending seems awesome. A fascinating volume, *George Washington's Expense Account* by Marvin Kitman, outlines these and other Washington expenses during the war. An admirer, Benedict Arnold (who later wrote the commander-in-chief a letter of apology that sought to explain the reason for his treason), went deeply into debt attempting to imitate Washington's life-style.

On his election as President, Washington once again offered Congress to serve without salary and be reimbursed for expenses only. Shaken, the heads of state begged him to accept instead the generous salary of $25,000 a year. That decision undoubtedly saved the young nation a small fortune.

CHAPTER III

The Young Nation

Some history texts tell us a great and glorious American nation emerged to prominence as the Revolution ended. Not true. Instead, the world witnessed a sad display of dissidence and in-fighting. For, as soon as they gained their freedom, the 13 feeble new "nations" began quarreling bitterly among themselves. And their inability to bargain with foreign powers caused them to be treated with the international disdain accorded small or impotent nations. The new states drifted toward what appeared to be chaos and ultimate anarchy.

Many observers in Europe believed, often with satisfaction, that the 13 new American states and their alliance, the Confederation, would soon collapse. When the impending fall occurred, the watchful Europeans planned to move in and divide the shattered colonies among themselves. But a startling phenomenon occurred—a second revolution, this one bloodless, replaced America's existing system of government with a different form of government. This sudden overthrow was achieved peacefully by extra-legal means. In a nation where violence has often been synonymous with problem-solving, the bloodless revolution which established the Constitution of the United States looms as perhaps an ideal model of how change can be effected successfully.

Prior to the adoption of the Constitution, the United States, operating under the Articles of Confederation, was not a "nation" in the modern sense of the word. It was a confederation, an alliance among thirteen independent and sovereign nation-states. This league merely served as an administrative bond among the separate territories. The Confederated alliance was somewhat like a modern nation in that it could declare war against an outside invader, but it had no power to force the individual states to comply. If a state chose to remain neutral in the wake of the Confederation's act it could do so. The *Articles of Confederation* established a "firm league of friendship" between the states which retained "sovereignty, freedom, and independence." Under the *Articles* no executive branch existed to implement laws and no coercive power extended over the states to assure their compliance.

The attempts to honor British treaty agreements demonstrated the impotence of America's new central government. In the peace settlement following the Revolution the United States agreed to pay its British creditors and to return seized Tory land, but these actions could only be recommended to the states. Though empowered to make treaties, the Confederation could not compel the states to observe them. The states, as independent nations, chose to not comply with the treaty, since they had not signed it. This refusal gave the British an excuse for continuing to maintain their forts in the Northwest. The British outposts were a growing source of irritation to the Americans, who nonetheless lacked the power to demand their removal. After the war Great Britain refused to enact a trade treaty with the Confederation, correctly pointing out that only by signing thirteen individual treaties could the pact succeed.

The British did not assign an ambassador to the new nation because its central government was so disorganized and feeble. The Spanish government, in its dealings with the United States, maintained an attitude of condescension and belligerence. Spain paid the Indians to attack the states and refused to open the Mississippi River at New Orleans to American vessels. Against these provocations Congress was powerless to act. Even its power to declare war was futile; needed troops and weaponry could be supplied only by the states.

Failure in dealing with foreign powers was only one of America's difficulties during the postwar years. Signs of ill-will erupted between the states, such as the boundary dispute between Connecticut and Pennsylvania. The two nearly went to war over the issue, and a similar feud between Vermont and New York sparked a call-out of troops. Fortunately the action halted short of full-scale war. Hostilities were also vented in trade restrictions and duties imposed by the states on one another, laws which served only to heighten enmity between the states. The weakness of the central government and the growing discord between the states portended certain doom for the alliance.

Another outgrowth of the weakness and confusion prevalent during the Confederation period was the farmers' rebellions. Economic conditions were poor throughout the country, with farmers being the hardest hit. Many lost their land to foreclosure. In 1786 "Shays' Rebellion" erupted, an uprising of organized farmers who succeeded in halting such foreclosures by forcibly preventing court sessions, and thus the foreclosure proceedings they conducted. The rebel farmers also released debtors from the prisons and prevented the convening of the state supreme court. State troops were unable to quell the insurrection for nearly six months. Similar disturbances occurred in Vermont and New Hampshire, further signs of the spreading discontent and the inability of the Confederation either to keep order or stabilize the economic forces which had triggered the rebellion. As before, the legislature surrendered to the demands of the rebels.

Compounding the post-revolution crisis, the economies of the 13 states were soon plunged into severe depression. The governments freely printed currencies to pay their debts, and this paper soon became worthless. Thousands of farmers lost their land, while countless others were imprisoned for inability to meet their debts. Western settlers spoke of seceding from the Confederation because they needed passage rights along the Mississippi, and the Confederation could not gain this concession from Spain. Responsible men grew desperate and began to actively seek change, yet the prevailing fear of a strong central government blocked their efforts for change. Washington declared, "We are fast verging to anarchy and confusion."

A group of prominent men soon moved to prevent this. They

convened at Philadelphia in 1787 in an effort to remake the government. The smaller farmers, wage-earners and frontier settlers were not represented at this Constitutional convention; the delegates were powerful politicians, wealthy landowners and businessmen, and others of education and stature. They had been appointed by their respective states to improve and amend the *Articles*. Instead, the Convention went without authority beyond this charge and wholly discarded the *Articles*. They soon began drafting a completely new plan of government, justifying their actions beyond the power delegated them and stating that, no matter what the fruits of their efforts, the individual states would be free to adopt or reject their recommendations. Certainly the need for a complete change was evident. Four months later the Convention finished its work. Only three of the forty-two delegates refused to approve the document which emerged. It was sent to the states for ratification.

Those who had formed this Constitution acted extralegally in still another way. The *Articles of Confederation* stated as a requirement the unanimous vote of all member states in the alliance before an amendment could be enacted. But the new Constitution was to go into effect after only nine states had approved it, thereby circumventing the requirements laid down in the *Articles of Confederation*. Yet it was a necessary bold stroke if a stable and effective government was to be achieved.

After fierce legislative fighting in many states, the Constitution was ratified by the required number. By this second revolution the alliance was transformed into a true nation of unified states. Thus, in a very real sense, the birth of the United States of America occurred not in 1776 but in 1788.

Yet all 13 states did not voluntarily ratify the new Constitution. New York, North Carolina, and Rhode Island held out, fearing the magnitude of the power the new central government would wield, power far exceeding that which the king and Parliament had possessed and which the colonists had found repressive. Finally, New York voted its approval, fearful the eastern sector of that state otherwise would secede and join the Union. North Carolina did not ratify the Constitution until a year later. Tiny Rhode Island resisted, an independent state surrounded by a new unified nation. The Union soon brought pressure to bear on Rhode Island, threatening to treat her as a foreign nation. Finally she too joined, in 1790. The new American nation under the Constitution began functioning officially in 1789, and its new government was soon guiding the course of all the states.

As one of its first official actions, the new government broke the Alliance of 1778, among the earliest treaties signed during the Revolution. Ever since that fateful decision, America's role in treaties has been as notorious in the breach as in the observance. Though countless treaties have been signed by the United States, they have been as much ignored as heeded.

Thus it was that, in 1778, the United States signed a treaty with France, pledging to defend French territories "forever against all other powers." But entering a war to defend the French in time of need would have been very difficult for the new country. And so, in 1793, Washington issued a proclamation of neutrality, which in effect made the treaty with France invalid. The United States had chosen to ignore her pledge and her moral obligation in favor of her own welfare. Though clearly it was expedient, and perhaps even wise for the young nation to retract her treaty promises, Americans should not be deluded into thinking their homeland is above such actions.

The young nation faced a whole spectrum of crises in the years following its inception—crises which severely tested, but also tempered and strengthened her. One was an incident similar to "Shays' Rebellion," aptly named the Whiskey Rebellion, which erupted in Pennsylvania in 1794. It was led by a group of farmers and distillers in revolt against the newly-enacted liquor tax. The group rioted and drove the tax collectors out of their respective counties. President Washington, under the powers accorded him in the new Constitution, called out 12,000 troops. The rebellion was quelled quickly without a single shot being fired. Thereafter its leaders were brought to trial and convicted, though pardons later were granted by the President. The whole incident, in contrast to the Shays affair, demonstrated that with the strong national government there no longer was cause to fear the rise of anarchy. Washington had been able to call up more troops to subdue this insurrection than he ever had commanded at one time during the Revolution. Such massive display of force probably was the key reason the revolt was peacefully quelled without bloodshed. Widespread public fears of the new government's power began to subside as it demonstrated the stability it could achieve.

Washington's tenure in office symbolized to the young republic the strength of its newly-conceived government. Yet he ruled wth the pomp and austerity of the English kings, so much so that few were at ease in his presence. Washington declined to shake hands with anyone, as was the new-world custom, but insisted on the formal bow. His life-style was modeled on that of the Old World aristocracy. He rode the streets in a grand carriage and maintained many exquisitely uniformed servants. His total bearing was that of a royal figurehead rather than the dynamic leader of a young nation. When he expressed the desire to be called "His Mightiness, the President of the United States," the Speaker of the House dissolved into laughter. The sensitive first President never forgave him.

Washington loathed having thrust upon him those duties of office he did not desire to perform. While President he proclaimed that he would rather be on his farm than "be made emperor of the world," and on another occasion, "I would rather be in my grave than in the Presidency." Because of his distaste for the duties of his office Washington permitted Jefferson and Hamilton wide latitude of action. Fortunately for the young republic, both were very able men, though often at odds. Hamilton succeeded brilliantly as Secretary of the Treasury, but fought continually with Jefferson, then Secretary of State.

Washington's knowledge of economics, diplomacy and political science was extremely limited compared to that of his able Secretaries. He sat mutely at Cabinet meetings listening to Jefferson and Hamilton argue at length. It was unfortunate that Washington chose to consult Jefferson on finance and Hamilton on foreign affairs, a contrary course that led chiefly to confusion. He failed to provide strong leadership.

Foreign diplomatic problems threatened the new nation. America's relations with France grew steadily worse after she broke the treaty with the French government. Formerly she and France had been steadfast allies. Most Americans sympathized with the cause of the French Revolution. Washington's neutrality caused a rift between France and America, which grew when French ships began attacking American trading vessels. In 1796 the relationship between the two powers had deteriorated to the extent that war with France seemed imminent. In just a few short years America's closest ally had become her enemy. A call for a declaration of war against France by President John Adams doubtless would have received wide popular support, so intense had anti-French feelings become throughout America. Normally reasonable and responsible men advocated war, and, inflamed by the passions which were arousing the nation, began militantly to prepare for it.

The incident which triggered the widespread desire for war was a relatively minor one. France had shrugged when her privateers attacked American ships, irritated at America's announced neutrality and, more recently, at the treaty America had signed with Britain. When privately-owned French ships continued to attack American merchant vessels, President Adams dispatched several federal officials to negotiate with France. The French foreign minister, Talleyrand, however, stipulated a sizeable bribe be paid by the Americans as the fee for halting the acts of aggression. The American envoys refused to pay, and soon an irate American public was clamoring "Millions for defense, but not one cent for tribute!"

As was often to be the case, the American people had enlarged a minor, mundane incident into one fraught with challenges and stirring the highest ideals. The American envoys doubtless would have paid Talleyrand his bribe, except that they did not trust him to fulfill his pledge. Indeed at that very time, America was paying a yearly tribute to the Barbary states as ransom against attack by Barbary pirate ships.

Talleyrand's demand aroused such national righteousness that Americans soon were willing to go to war over it. But

Adams stood firm against war, Talleyrand eventually backed off, and senseless bloodshed was averted. This truly was John Adams' finest hour.

In 1798 Congress, still riding the crest of pro-war passions, enacted a series of repressive laws called the Alien and Sedition Acts. These measures were aimed both at silencing dissenters against governmental policies and at controlling foreign immigrants in the wake of anti-foreigner sentiments aroused by the threat of war. Mistrust and prejudice against foreigners were manifest in the Alien Act, which empowered the President to expel those resident aliens and non-citizens he deemed dangerous to the peace and security of the United States. This deportation process required no trial, merely the President's signature. The act stirred great resentment and fear among aliens as it denied their right to trial by jury, a human right formerly accorded all throughout America. Though President Adams never invoked the law, several shiploads of French aliens voluntarily returned to France out of fear of what otherwise might befall them. New legislation also empowered the President to deport or imprison aliens almost at will during time of war.

The Sedition Act struck directly at freedom seemingly guaranteed in the Constitution. This law, wholly disregarding the tenet of free speech set forth in the Bill of Rights, made criticism of government officials illegal and punishable. The Federalist Party then in power used it to silence opposition criticism at election time. Twenty-five persons were charged with violating the law and ten were convicted, including the editors of opposition newspapers. Since those early days of the Republic few laws have been enacted which were as blatantly repressive of Constitutional rights. Fortunately they expired several years later and were not renewed.

Another enlightening episode in the development of the young Republic was that of tribute money paid to the Barbary pirates. During the terms of President Washington and Adams, the United States paid various potentates of regions along the North African coast to help ensure the safe passage of ships on the Mediterranean, an area infested with pirates.

The latter, operating out of bases in North Africa's Barbary states, attacked foreign merchant ships of any nation that declined to pay the stipulated annual tribute. Many nations, including the United States, found paying the tribute less costly in terms of lives and money than risking pirate attack. Between 1790 and 1800, the United States paid over two million dollars in such tributes to the Barbary pirates, a prudent approach if not a very courageous one.

When Jefferson assumed the Presidency the immorality of these payments loomed counter to his principles, and when the Pasha of Tripoli increased the stated fees, Jefferson refused to sanction the payments altogether. He dispatched warships to the Mediterranean, determined to unleash a show of force against the extortionists and protect American ships against their attack. Tripoli reciprocated by declaring war on the United States, and a series of battles ensued, resulting at last in the humiliation of the United States and her subsequent resumption of tribute payments.

At first America's warships merely escorted her merchant vessels through the Mediterranean, but then they attempted a naval blockade of Tripoli, with the emboldened Americans even pursuing Tripolitan ships. The results of this undeclared war by the Americans were disappointing, compared to their noble purpose. America, unable to rout Tripoli, eventually signed a treaty favorable to her foe and paid a large sum to the pasha at the close of the conflict, continuing to pay tribute fees for another decade.

One historian has described this foray, which might be regarded as America's first war, as "halfhearted and ill-starred." The thirty-six gun frigate, *Philadelphia*, chasing an enemy ship came too close to shore, became grounded on a reef, and was forced to surrender. The pirates seized the crew of three hundred as prisoners and kept the large American vessel for their own. The Tripolitan port was well-fortified against the American attacks which proved fruitless. Though American fighting men displayed unusual courage and became legend in years to follow, their attack on the port ranked as a dismal failure. Another attack, across the desert, was launched against Tripoli but also failed.

In 1805 America signed a peace treaty with Tripoli which reinstated the bribes against which the American public had rallied. The ideal for which the war had been fought was abandoned in the wake of defeat. Tribute to Tripoli, as well as to the other three Barbary states, continued until the small North African territories began to weaken under the growing control of colonizing European powers. The British takeover of Malta in 1814 was the beginning of the end, terminating in the French occupation of Algeria in 1830.

The early years of the American republic produced one of its most well-known archtraitors, Aaron Burr, third Vice-President of the United States. Burr's infamy was first revealed during the election of 1800, in which Thomas Jefferson, a Republican, challenged the Federalist incumbent, President John Adams. Jefferson defeated Adams by a narrow margin but failed to garner the needed margin of electoral votes for the Presidency. Burr, his vice-presidential running-mate, received the identical number of electoral votes, since the two had run together on the same ticket and since all Republicans had cast their votes faithfully for the two Republican candidates. While the electors clearly intended that Jefferson be President, the system (later corrected by the Twelfth Amendment) made the meaning of the tie-vote confusing. Further, Burr refused to step aside and yield the title to Jefferson, as would an honorable man. Because of the tie-vote the issue went automatically to the House of Representatives for decision (one of only two times in the nation's history that the Presidency was decided in this way). Hamilton, though long a bitter enemy of Jefferson, recognized him as the true choice of the electors. He thus endorsed and supported Jefferson, who finally was elected on the thirty-sixth ballot. It was ironic, yet also a tribute to Hamilton, that he had helped elect his foe to the Presidency of the United States. During his term as Vice-President, Burr, whose actions had been so dishonorable in the election, was never again trusted by President Jefferson.

In 1804 he was cast aside by Jefferson when the latter chose a new running mate.

Shunned by the party regulars in Washington, Burr ran for the Governorship of New York. A group of men called the Essex Junta were advocating that New England secede from the Union and create a new nation, a "Northern Confederacy." The plan first called for capturing political control of New York. For this purpose the Junta approached candidate Burr, who gave the conspirators tacit encouragement. Though Burr probably did not agree to be a party to their plans, neither did he reject them. Instead, he accepted their help without publicly committing himself to their scheme. Hamilton worked feverishly against Burr's election, and many acrimonious words were exchanged in writing by the two during the campaign. On election day Hamilton publicly exposed the plot of the Essex Junta, and Burr consequently lost the election. For the second time Burr had been a party to unscrupulous dealings, and for the second time Hamilton had achieved Burr's defeat. Burr, now obsessed by hatred for Hamilton, challenged the first Secretary of the Treasury to a duel. Hamilton, whose son had been killed in a duel, disapproved of dueling yet felt his honor was at stake. He resolved not to use the weapon but let himself be shot. The duelists met on July 11, 1804. True to his resolve Hamilton never raised his weapon. He was wounded mortally and died soon afterward. This tragic end of one of America's greatest leaders simultaneously branded the nation's former vice-president as a murderer.

The villainous Aaron Burr was to give rise to even further infamy. Wanted for murder by authorities in New York and New Jersey, he fled to Philadelphia. While still Vice-President Burr had committed treason by offering the British ambassador in Washington a plan to "effect a separation of the Western part of the United States." For this purpose he asked the British for funds, as well as naval support at the mouth of the Mississippi. The British refused aid. Several years later Burr proceeded unassisted in his plan. All of his aims are not known, but he clearly wanted to establish an empire in the West with himself as sovereign. Whether he intended to seize the desired

54

territory from Spain or the United States also is uncertain. Probably he envisioned seizing all or part of Mexico by force. His new empire would grow when western states seceded from the Union to join it. The capitol, he determined, would be at New Orleans. Only one thing is clear: it was a treasonous plan of grandiose magnitude. Burr assembled a small army on the Ohio River, planning to move on and capture either Mexico or New Orleans. Though Jefferson knew of this plan, he did nothing to stop it, perhaps willing to forego interference if the group limited its attacks to and designs on Spanish territory. Finally when one of the conspirators revealed the plot to Jefferson just before it was slated to go into effect, Jefferson was forced to act. He issued an order for Burr's arrest and warned the nation to be on guard against the treasonous band. Burr was arrested while trying to escape to Spanish Florida and brought to trial.

President Jefferson, under whom Burr had served as Vice President only three years earlier, personally assisted the prosecution at Burr's trial, so deep had his hatred of Burr become. He even offered an automatic pardon to anyone willing to testify against Burr, and a French adventurer involved in the conspiracy was promised a U.S. Army commission if he would testify against Burr. Jefferson had knowingly allowed the conspiracy to develop, halting it only at the last minute. Why he waited so long is unclear, but his vindictiveness toward Burr at the trial was apparent. Conversely, Chief Justice Marshall, an enemy of Jefferson, showed favoritism to Burr, whose trial evolved more into a political affair than an impartial service to objective justice. In his instructions to the jury Marshall defined treason in such a way that Burr could not be found guilty. Thus acquitted, Burr fled to Europe to escape prosecution for the murder of Hamilton still pending in several states. While in exile he planned a conspiracy to conquer Florida. Though Burr still had visions of empire, Napoleon could see little personal advantage in the plot and declined aid. Burr finally returned to America years later and quietly practiced law for the remainder of his life. But irony stalked him even to his deathbed. His last wife, Eliza, divorced him the day he died, thereby forfeiting a large inheritance. Burr who had spent his life seeking power, had won only historical infamy.

Several other events transpired during Jefferson's Presidency which helped shape the future of America. His administration gained from one stroke of fortune, Napoleon's offer to sell the Louisiana Territory, a land area which on its acquisition nearly doubled the size of the United States. This fortuitous event is often termed the greatest achievement of Jefferson's administration.

A second important event under Jefferson was his attack upon the federal judiciary, the failure of which made clear that the judicial branch of government would remain independent. Jefferson's assault had been partisan in nature. The President was angered at the large number of judges the Federalists had appointed just before leaving office. These "midnight judges," so-called because President Adams reportedly had stayed up until midnight frantically signing their commissions on his last day in office, all were Federalists, and Jefferson greatly resented their appointments. He set out to deflate the power of the courts by impeaching some of the judges, thereby asserting his control over the courts, a dangerous precedent had he accomplished his goal. The President's first attack, in which he refused to distribute a number of judicial appointments already signed by Adams, brought him into direct confrontation with the Supreme Court. Rather than summoning the President—a move which would have undermined the courts, for Jefferson undoubtedly would have refused to comply with the court order—Chief Justice Marshall instead declared unconstitutional an act of Congress around which the case revolved. Marshall thereby avoided a direct engagement with the President and at the same time established the precedent that the Supreme Court could nullify federal laws found to conflict with the Constitution. Jefferson's attack had given Marshall a singular opportunity to strengthen the judiciary, and this infuriated the President.

Jefferson then focused his wrath upon Pickering, an alcoholic and incompetent judge who clearly was unfit for his position. The impeachment proceedings against Pickering were swift, and the judge was removed from the bench. But the President's next target, Samuel Chase, an associate justice of the Supreme Court, did not appear incompetent. Though he had delivered a number of controversial rulings, his judicial conduct fell far short of the Constitutional criteria of "high crimes and misdemeanors" on which removal of a Supreme Court judge must be based. Thus the Senate refused the President's bid to remove Chase, thereby checking Jefferson's vindictive attack on the judiciary before it could gather further impetus. Thereafter, the independence of the federal courts was more secure.

The War of 1812, which concluded this youthful phase of American history, was not a spectacular finale. America's irrationality in entering the war was exceeded only by her ineptness in fighting it. Fortunately, relatively few men were killed. America was not victorious and barely held her own in the senseless combat. Except for the grim note of battle deaths, this war might otherwise have gone down in history as a slapstick comedy.

The numerous factors which triggered the War of 1812 were led off by the British practice of "impressment." Under British law, in time of national emergency neutral ships could be stopped by the Royal Navy and searched for English subjects, who then could be "impressed," that is, taken aboard the British ship and forced to work. England at the time was embroiled in a great war against Napoleon and needed every able-bodied British citizen she could muster to man her large naval fleet. Napoleon dominated most of the European continent, and the British, who ruled the seas, hoped to blockade him into surrender.

The British, as well as the French, warned they would seize all neutral ships trading with the enemy. Together they captured nearly 1,500 American ships. American merchants were willing to risk such shipping losses because the profits made when a ship did get through were so huge that they offset the losses involved.

Impressment may not have been the fairest of practices, but it also was not the worst. There were 10,000 or more Englishmen sailing on American ships at the time. British sailors posed as Americans to qualify for the higher wages paid aboard United States ships. Many of them carried forged citizenship papers.

In 1807 a major instance of impressment occurred. The captain of the British ship *Leopard*, knowing English deserters were aboard the United States frigate *Chesapeake*, stopped the American ship and demanded their delivery. When the American captain denied any British were aboard, the *Leopard* opened fire. Three were killed, eighteen wounded, and the British deserters were taken captive. The Crown denounced the act of the British captain and offered reparations. But the incident aroused many Americans against the British. The English were equally aroused that Americans would harbor known British deserters. Several years later, the incident reversed itself when an American frigate, the *President*, launched an unprovoked attack upon a British vessel. The little British sloop was demolished and 32 Englishmen were killed or wounded.

Though it can be seen that the transgressions leading up to the War of 1812 were not all British, of the 5,000 sailors impressed between 1803 and 1812 some were naturalized American citizens. The United States claimed her naturalized citizens were Americans, exempt from British dominance. But Britain, who claimed they nonetheless remained British subjects, refused to recognize naturalization as a change in citizenship. Thus the heated dispute went on, each side contending it was right. England regarded those she was impressing as English subjects and maintained this irritating procedure was necessary because of a manpower crisis. America was infuriated over the stopping of her ships and even angrier when a case of impressment involving a naturalized American came to light. Though American shippers were profiting tremendously from the European war, America openly protested the British blockade. This national anger smoldered until it flared into full-scale war. Yet it was a war without real cause, since Great Britain posed no threat to the United States. Both British impressment and the blockade were differences that could have been resolved, and both subsided when the war against Napoleon ended.

In fact, just at the time the United States declared war, British maritime policy was changing to a more favorable attitude toward her. Had the United States delayed the call to war but a short time, she would have learned Parliament had voted to discontinue the use of impressment. The action was one of American pride, neither vital to her defense nor crucial to her interests. As such it proved a costly error.

Napoleon, on the other hand, posed a real threat to United States security. Probably he would have attempted to conquer America had it not been for the British Navy, its major barrier against French aggression. This clear threat was obvious to the British, who could not fathom America's desire to aid a man who might one day seek to add it to his burgeoning empire. Still, shortsighted Americans continued trading with the French. The *London Times* noted in 1812,

> The Alps and the Appennines of America are the British Navy. If ever that should be removed, a short time will suffice to establish the headquarters of a French Duke-Marshall at Washington.

By declaring war on the British in 1812 America weakened them in their fight against Napoleon. She also risked self-destruction by engaging such a powerful European empire in combat. The year the United States invaded Canada with 5,000 troops, Napoleon marched into Russia with 500,000. Britain was like a swordman fighting a masterful opponent while simultaneously dallying an amateur with his left hand. The amateur, the United States, clearly had attacked the wrong opponent at the wrong time.

Considering that American maritime interests were supposedly damaged by Britain's acts at this time it is surprising that these interests opposed the war strenuously. They resented Britain's trespasses, but correctly saw that war would be far worse for them and for the nation than a patient waiting out of the European War, which would terminate unjust British maritime practices. Yet westerners strongly advocated war for several reasons. They believed it could mean the conquest of Canada, thus opening the rich region for American expansion. They also believed the British in Canada were inciting Indian attacks upon the American frontier. The British in fact had refused to aid Indian uprisings and had tried to calm them. The true cause underlying the Indian aggression was the greed and avarice of the frontiersmen. Yet America's fervor for war against Britain continued.

Also motivating the West's call for war was the prevailing agricultural depression. Frustrated and angry, the frontiersmen vented their aggression against the British, who in no way had caused the depression: it was an outgrowth of the West's inept but expensive transportation system. Yet the farmers blamed the depression on the English blockade, and the West's cry for war soon was chorused by thousands in the South. Thus the Hawks, rallying more against depression and Indian hostilities than against Britain's maritime laws, talked Congress and the nation into war. But the United States did not enter the war with unanimity. Strong opposition continued from the New England states, and the Federalists even drafted a counter-declaration declaring the war unjust.

Further, once the conflict began, even Western enthusiasm waned. The war was met chiefly with nationwide indifference, with only a small number willing to make the sacrifices required. As in the Revolution, a vast number of Americans believed the war was wrong.

Generalship of the War of 1812 was inadequate on both sides, but several instances of American incompetence were exceptional. America's military inability compounded by grave shortages of volunteers to fill the ranks resulted in an army hardly capable of waging organized war.

The initial campaigns were disastrous. Congress authorized the recruitment of 25,000 troops, but the response was dismal. Only about one-fourth that number came forward and the reaction to the war in other respects was equally unenthusiastic. Probably more money was lent by America's Northern money merchants to the English during the war than to America's Federal Treasury. New England farmers shipped vast food stores to Canada, much of which went directly to the British Army. U.S. General William Hull, an inveterate braggart, marched his men to Detroit, believing the Canadians would immediately desert at the sight of his army. Instead, the Canadians took chase after Hull and he surrendered before a shot ever was fired.

The war seemed to be an opportunity to "liberate" Canada and annex it to the United States. But the Canadians viewed the "liberation" effort as an unjust invasion of their country. Another American invasion of Canada was attempted at Fort Niagara. There the American forces were beaten badly by an overwhelming number of Canadians, while the New York militia looked on from across the Niagara River, refusing to fight outside their state. A third American invasion of Canada was led by the most imposing figure of the war, General Henry Dearborn, who insisted on being transported in a specially-designed cart. Needless to say this hale fellow led no charges personally, but contented himself with verbal command of his troops. When his troops reached the border enroute to Montreal and staunchly refused to cross it, Dearborn turned his cart and his army around and returned to camp.

Many Americans had believed Canada would fall before their army's show of force, but the attempted invasion of Canada failed, and the Canadians were soon moving into Ohio. Others believed the Canadians would be sympathetic to and aid the United States, but the former resented being attacked unjustly because of British wrongdoings. Thus the Canadians rallied spiritedly against the Americans. Even today, the War of 1812 is regarded by many Canadians as an unprovoked invasion of their land in which they fought valiantly to stave off the hostile Americans. Canada had not impressed America's sailors nor seized her ships and regarded the invasion of her soil as wholly unjustified. The Canadians fought with tenacity and furor, hurling back the invading American forces.

Though the American military fared somewhat better in several later campaigns, the capture of America's Capitol at Washington, D.C. by the British proved especially humiliating. The British forces marching on Washington were met at Bladensburg, on the outskirts of the Capitol, by an American army twice their size, led by General William Winder. While President Madison and other federal officials watched with obvious pride, the large American Army confronted the small British contingent. Several shots were fired and Winder's army turned and ran. A British officer later recalled, "No troops could behave worse than they did." Madison watched the Capitol buildings burn to the ground as the American Army fled from a handful of British soldiers.

At the Battle of New Orleans, the American forces fought under Andrew Jackson. The Americans performed well, dealing the British heavy casualties. The battle would have been recorded as a splendid American victory except that it was waged after the war was over. The British-American peace treaty already had been signed. Those who fell at New Orleans died without cause, although the Battle has been hailed in some texts as a great American victory.

By 1814, America was weary of the war and happy to sue for peace. Some Americans had fought bravely. Many others had refused to participate. Most Americans were relieved to see the war end though the treaty did not fulfill one U.S. objective. Though many battles had been lost, the peace treaty did not extract a heavy toll from America since the British, too, had fought ineffectively. The prewar situation was restored with America even dropping its demand for an end to impressment. In all, the War of 1812 was a senseless event which most were glad to resolve and many to forget.

CHAPTER IV

War on Mexico

For America, the War of 1812 was militarily indecisive and the peace treaty which it effected wrought no significant changes. Yet from it emerged a redirection of national focus: a turning-away from Europe and a deepening concentration upon affairs within the Western Hemisphere which were to prevail for the next hundred years. The war also generated a surge of nationalism throughout a republic whose citizens previously had reserved their major allegiances to their native states. The Monroe Doctrine in 1823 illustrated how greatly America's nationalistic sentiments and her new spirit of independence from Europe had grown since the Revolution. The election of Andrew Jackson to the Presidency symbolized this new nationalistic concept in which all segments of the population—rich and poor, rural and urban, Northern, Eastern, Western and Southern—would participate together in democracy. Despite Jackson's great popularity, however, events which occurred during his administration contributed to growing divisiveness within the young nation, and culminating finally in civil war.

Thus the nationalism which grew to its peak after the War of 1812 endured only a short time before the nation again was divided by deepening sectional conflicts. Slavery, tariffs, the debate over the Bank of the United States—these and other issues sharply divided the nation along sectional lines, fomenting widespread public unrest. Jackson's administration dominated the most important years between the War of 1812 and the Mexican-American War in shaping America's future. While

Jackson openly patronized the spoils system by firing several thousand federal employees, replacing them with people who had supported his campaign, his election represented the rise of the "common man" to the helm of power in government. But the sectional disunity that erupted during his administration drew America into conflict and chaos.

John C. Calhoun, vice-president under Jackson, resigned his office to lead the growing nullification movement in South Carolina. This movement, encouraged by Jackson's support of Georgia's nullification of a U.S. Supreme Court decision, advocated the right of states to nullify laws enacted by Congress, utilizing as its test case America's recently enacted tariff laws. Congress reacted by reducing the tariffs, and Jackson initiated military preparations at the last minute. Crisis and civil war were averted as compromises were effected on both sides. The tariff issue itself was not important enough to precipitate civil war, but the nullification crisis reflected the extreme sectional differences that jeopardized the preservation of the Union as early as 1832.

Jackson left office a living legend, his popularity greatest in the West and among the less privileged. He had strengthened the Presidency, but in doing so had run roughshod over Congress and the Supreme Court, destroying the balance of power among the three. Since Jackson's power was linked almost entirely to his personal magnetism, his departure from office left the Presidency a weaker role. Congress reacted to his past dictatorialism by seizing the reins of government, so that all the Presidents succeeding Jackson up to Lincoln were totally overshadowed by the legislature.

Jackson lacked both political experience and knowledge of the issues of his day, his popularity stemming primarily from his celebrated military achievements. He thus made many errors in executive decisions which generated havoc and undermined the young nation. Perhaps his most serious error in judgment was his treatment of the Cherokee Indians. He refused to implement the decision of the Supreme Court in the case of *Worcester* vs. *Georgia,* that crimes committed within Cherokee territory should be tried by Indian courts, a right already guaranteed by the U.S. in several treaties with the Cherokee. Jackson flatly refused to enforce this decision, the President's duty according to the Constitution. His legendary reply was "John Marshall has made his decision. Now let him enforce it." Also to his detriment Jackson embraced the spoils system, filling government offices on a large scale with friends, cronies, campaign supporters, and other party comrades, many of whom were lacking in integrity. He placed loyalty to friends above efficiency and ability in office. But an even graver error in judgment was his destruction of the Bank of the United States, which created instability in the economy that was to prevail for over a century. Though the Bank had been sorely in need of control, Jackson instead destroyed it and then proposed nothing to replace it. The major victims of this were the farmers and the poor, the very people whose interests Jackson purported to represent.

The factors leading to his destruction of the Bank were numerous and complex. Nicholas Biddle, president of the Bank, had a keen understanding of banking and finance. He adopted policies which, though unpopular among many segments of the populace, served to stabilize the national economy. Biddle knew the Bank of the United States could control the sharp fluctuations of the business cycle by regulating the availability of credit throughout the nation. Though he was a brilliant financier, his policies angered many, some because they limited their profits, and others, notably the farmers, because they placed a ceiling on the amount of capital they could borrow. Many farmers did not realize that liberal loans spurred overproduction, which sent commodity prices into a tailspin and could lead to agricultural depression. Indeed, most of the opposition to Bank policies, including the overt animosity of the President, was linked to an ignorance of basic economics.

Jackson's irrational loathing of the Bank was so intense that he decided to effect its closure several years before the natural expiration of its charter by law. To achieve this he ordered withdrawal of all federal monies from the Bank and their deposit into various state banks. By law only the Secretary of the Treasury could remove federal funds. Treasury Secretary Louis McLane refused to do so, recognizing Jackson's order as foolhardy. Jackson promoted McLane to Secretary of State, then appointed William Duane Secretary of the Treasury. But Jackson had neglected to first ask Duane his views on the Bank funds withdrawal. Duane, like McLane, realized the inadvisability of transferring the funds to state banks and refused to do so. Jackson fired Duane and appointed a third Secretary of the Treasury, who did as he commanded.

Jackson's contempt for the courts, earlier made clear in the Cherokee case, was again in evidence in his closing of the Bank of the United States. In its ruling on *McCulloch* vs. *Maryland*, the U.S. Supreme Court declared the Bank to be Constitutional, but Jackson disregarded this decision and declared the Bank unconstitutional, explaining that as President his duty was to support the Constitution as he saw it. But Jackson's fervor to crush the Bank reaped a bitter harvest, starting with a seven-year depression that began in 1837. For the next 100 years the United States' financial system was chaotic, and depressions rode their course unabated by the stabilizing influence a strong national bank could have exerted.

Jackson also demonstrated poor judgment in guiding America's relations with France and England, nearly plunging the nation into war with France. In his diplomatic dealings with both countries he took drastic risks to win petty victories. In one such instance, when France failed to pay a debt to the United States, Jackson spoke wildly of "reprisals upon French property" and "taking redress into our own hands," threats which triggered irresponsible talk of war in France. Had war erupted, the President's rashness could have cost the nation dearly. Thus while Jackson's positive contributions were numerous his errors were equal in their magnitude.

Before America's growing sectional rift triggered the Civil War, another dark event—the Mexican-American War—intensified sectional differences. Conflicts over slavery in the new territories raised by that unjust war made it but part of a larger conflict leading to the tragic 1860's. Yet it also had great significance in its own right.

The annexation of Texas and the subsequent Mexican-American War were blemishes on the annals of the young nation. The giant exodus of Americans into Texas, to settle there in large numbers, soon precipitated a revolution against Mexico. Because the American settlers, rather than the United States government wrested Texas from Mexico, this sorry event often is referred to as a case of "backdoor aggression." Then, after existing as an independent republic for a decade, Texas was annexed officially to the United States. President Polk, not satisfied even by this vast land grab, spurred the United States into a war with Mexico—a war that was to gain California and New Mexico as its main prizes.

The real motivation of the Mexican-American War, imperialist greed for land, was obvious to all the world. The events of "manifest destiny" spurred a tremendous territorial expansion for the United States, but the harvest was soon to prove a mixed blessing. It generated among Latin Americans fear and resentment of the United States, an alienation which continues to this day. The annexation of new territory aggravated the black slavery question, eventually erupting into the American Civil War, in which Mexico indirectly gained revenge against her greedy Northern neighbor.

The United States had coveted Texas from an early date, even claiming that it was part of the ill-defined Louisiana Purchase. When America purchased Florida from Spain in 1819, the U.S. agreed to relinquish her dubious claim to Texas. This angered greedy American expansionists. Westerners and others throughout the nation sharply criticized the federal government for withdrawing the Texas claim. They resolved to one day secure the area for the United States, a resolution that soon was to be ruthlessly carried out.

Mexico, which gained independence from Spain in 1821, wanted the vast rich Texas territory to grow and develop. Thus it followed the policy of offering free tracts of land to new settlers, encouraging Americans to migrate there. In their desire to see Texas develop and prosper, the Mexicans failed to foresee the new problms the immigrants would quickly incite. The Mexican government had set forth two prerequisites for immigration to Texas: conversion to Roman Catholicism and a pledge of loyalty to Mexico. American settlers ignored the first requisite from the outset, and the second was kept scarcely longer. The majority of settlers were Protestants who had no intention of converting to Catholicism but proved their lack of integrity by pledging to become Catholics for the lure of free land.

White American settlers flooded into Texas and, by 1830, there were some 30,000 in the territory. These settlers predominately were Anglo in descent, retaining their Protestant religion and English-speaking ways and flaunting many of the Mexican laws. They evaded Mexican import duties. Especially disturbing to the Mexicans was the heavy illegal influx of arms and munitions smuggled into Texas by the American settlers. They also evaded the Mexican law forbidding slavery by "freeing" their slaves at the border and then signing them to lifetime contracts as indentured servants.

The Mexican government was as worried by these infractions as by the constant talk of the United States annexing Texas and the desire of the ambitious, acquisitive Americans to "own" the entire continent. The American public and its newspapers made continuous reference to the inevitability of America's controlling the whole continent, and these speculations spread to the Mexican capital. Several abortive attempts by the United States government to purchase Texas, though flatly rejected by the Mexicans, made all too evident the ardent desire of the Americans to claim Texas as their own. One American envoy even attempted to buy Texas largely by tendering bribes to Mexican officials, and this generated additional ill-will toward the United States.

All of these factors led Mexico to slowly tighten her control of the territory, until, in 1830, she decreed an end to American immigration. But Mexico had not taken into account the Americans' rampant disregard for law as they continued to pour into Texas against the express orders of the Mexican government. As the illegal immigration continued Mexico's fears grew in intensity.

These infringements demanded an answer. In 1835, Mexico's opportunistic new dictator, Santa Anna, resolved to restore order in Texas and dispatched troops to halt the illegal American influx. His worst fears soon were confirmed when the whites rebelled. Unlike their Revolution against England, prefaced with lofty, high-sounding phrases, the Americans did not bother to dignify their uprising against Mexico. It was obvious they simply wanted control of the area. Nor had Mexico obstructed the inalienable rights of free men. She had not tread harshly upon the settlers nor grievously wronged them. She had, instead, given them free land and citizens' privileges. But the United States wanted Texas, and Mexico refused to sell it. There was only one alternative left—take it by force. Still, the United States government could not merely march in and seize control if it were to maintain any semblance of morality.

Naively, Mexico had provided the United States with just the right opportunity: her earlier invitation enabling any American to immigrate to Texas. For now, despite Mexico's reversal of the bid, Americans continued to pour in by the hundreds. Nor had she realized the required oath of loyalty would be taken so lightly by the incoming Americans. When the Mexican government at last realized its error, it was too late and no law could halt the huge influx of Americans into the rich fertile Texas area.

Revolution was not long in coming once the Americans had wrested a majority stature in Texas. Mexico dispatched armed forces in an attempt to enforce her laws and terminate the illegal influx of Americans, munitions, and slaves. When enforcement proved futile, martial law was declared. This proved to be the red flag which signaled the revolt.

At first the American settlers were poorly organized and could not even agree that independence was the most advantageous move for them. But shortly after fighting broke out the homesteading Americans united at last and declared their independence at Washington-on-the-Brazos in 1836. Immediately help poured in from the United States in the form of men, money, and arms. Cannons and supplies were shipped to the rebel army. Americans by the thousands moved across the border from every area of the United States, but especially from the South, to fight for Texas independence. The major part of the Texas Army was not composed of Texans, but of men and boys from the North, South, East and West who streamed into Texas just for the fight and would return to their homes, for the most part, after the foray. This vast number of non-Texans fighting for Texas independence is but one more reason the war was termed "backdoor aggression."

Meanwhile, the United States government, seeking to avoid involvement in a large, costly war with Mexico, officially declared its neutrality. What the United States government had failed to achieve through bribes and negotiations, its people accomplished forcefully through revolution. Although the United States was obligated by her proclamation of neutrality to keep American men and arms out of Texas, there is no evidence she tried to do so. If anything, her permissive, do-nothing attitude toward America's rebel forces signaled her silent consent.

As in the American Revolution, fighting began in small skirmishes and soon erupted into larger battles and ultimately, bloody, full-scale rebellion. The most famous battle, fought at the Alamo, is a testimony both to American and Mexican courage. Sam Houston, the general in charge of American forces, had ordered the troops to abandon San Antonio before the battle of the Alamo erupted because it would have been impossible to hold the town with the small force there. However, the troops, including Davy Crockett and Jim Bowie, stubbornly refused to leave their exposed position. The Mexicans fought courageously, risking almost certain death as they crossed the open distance around the fort and attempted to scale the high walls. Santa Anna called on the defenders of the Alamo to surrender, but they stubbornly refused. The Mexican general continued throwing hundreds of brave young men against the fortifications under tremendous enemy fire. Despite the mounting toll, the Mexican forces continued to press the attack. Eventually, they were victorious, at the cost of a thousand young lives. Because of their stubborn refusal to surrender, no American lives were spared within the Alamo. This bloody conquest helped weaken the Mexican Army and thereby hastened its defeat by the Americans at San Jacinto only six weeks later.

During the American rebellion, President Jackson had sent troops to the Texas border, allegedly to protect United States territory from stray combatants of either side. At one point General Gaines' army crossed into Mexican territory in clear violation of international neutrality laws. Since the Texas Army did not need the help of these U.S. forces, we can only speculate as to whether they would have intervened had the Texans been losing. And had the Mexican forces succeeded in routing the Texans and given chase, how would the U.S. militia have reacted when these forces approached the American border? Doubtless they would have permitted the Texas Army, largely composed of U.S. citizens, to cross the American border but would not have allowed the Mexicans to follow. This, too, would have violated national neutrality status.

In 1836, the Mexican Army was defeated at San Jacinto. Sam Houston had retreated in the wake of a Mexican offensive, but at San Jacinto he stopped and attacked the encamped Mexicans during their siesta. Many captives were taken including Santa Anna and the Mexican Army was driven from Texas soil. Though Mexico still refused to recognize the new independence of Texas, the settlers nevertheless declared the territory an independent republic.

The next step for the Texas settlers obviously was to seek annexation to the United States, a request President Jackson reluctantly refused because he was reluctant to trigger a full-scale war with Mexico. Nor did he want to fan the already heated slavery controversy by adding another slave state to the union. Jackson privately desired to annex Texas, but he believed a more propitious time would present itself.

The American settlers in Texas were sorely disappointed at the President's rejection after they had fought so bitterly to wrest Texas from the Mexicans. But Jackson's stand left them no alternative. They were forced to go their independent way for a decade, even flirting on occasion with Great Britain. During those ten years the Mexican government dispatched two military expeditions in an effort to reestablish its control over

Texas, which it still regarded as a Mexican territory. But in both instances the Mexican Army contented itself with attacking a single town, pillaging it, and then returning to Mexico. The massive Mexican attack expected and feared by the Americans never occurred. After almost a decade of independent home rule the United States at last considered Texas safe for annexation. The territory had been recognized as a nation by other world powers, and Mexico had made only meager attempts to reconquer her. Britain's friendly overtures to the new republic hastened the American move for annexation.

In 1844 presidential candidate James Polk campaigned on a bold, aggressive platform of expansionism, strongly advocating the admission of Texas and Oregon to the Union. Polk's platform urged the "re-annexation" of Texas, though it had never been annexed, and the "re-occupation" of Oregon, though it had never been occupied. Regarding the Oregon territory then in dispute with Britain, Polk's democratic supporters coined the slogan "Fifty-four forty or fight." His narrow margin of victory at the polls was seen as a "mandate" for manifest destiny, and even before Polk came into office, the outgoing President Tyler exerted pressure on Congress to approve the annexation of Texas. The Senate, however, defeated this expansionist issue, since many Northerners were fearful Texas would spark the rise of additional slave states. Tyler then presented the proposal to a joint session of the House and Senate, and annexation was approved at last by a narrow margin.

The new status of Texas increased the possibility of war. The United States hoped to stave off this outbreak through careful negotiations. Since Mexico had not attempted to reconquer Texas, the United States government believed she eventually would agree to sell her.

President Polk entered office in 1845, and an agreement soon was reached with Britain to fix the border through the Oregon territory at the 49th Parallel. Polk deftly maneuvered out of the uncompromising demand of his former campaign slogan: the 54th Parallel or war. Though the Oregon compromise averted war with Britain, it wasn't long before Polk incited war against Mexico. To countless Americans he was the living embodiment of "Manifest Destiny," the growing national belief that the United States was inhabited by God's chosen people, who, by His providence, would soon inhabit the entire continent. It was a notion not unlike the Germanic Super-Race concept of Nietzsche, which later was adopted in part by Hitler and fired the Nazi-Aryan philosophy. And James Knox Polk was its ideal exponent, a man who knew—and got—what he wanted.

Polk opened negotiations to purchase Texas, but he also wanted the Mexican territories of California and New Mexico (which then comprised the area that today are the six Southwestern states). Purchasing these prime areas was the President's first choice, but failing that he would settle for a rebellion in California or all-out war. The Mexicans staunchly refused to sell any of the territories, though there were several intimations they would ultimately consider selling Texas, since they no longer had control of it. Polk could have waited for a shift in Mexican public opinion, which would have spurred that government to proceed with negotiations. In the interim, he could have contented himself with the knowledge that Texas was firmly in American hands. But Polk was angry at Mexico's proud, persistent refusals and fearful as well that Britain would grab California. He decided upon more drastic measures, and his orders led directly to war with Mexico.

Polk's growing fear that he would lose California prompted decisive action. He dispatched a secret message to Americans in California, hinting that they should rebel against Mexican rule as Texas had done. He assured them of the United States' good will toward them if they decided upon this course. His intimation to the California settlers that they would be admitted into the Union once they gained independence was clearly unconstitutional, since only Congress can ratify such a measure. Nonetheless Polk sent naval ships to the California coast to be in readiness should a revolution erupt. His most extreme step, however, was taken in Texas. General Zachary Taylor and his forces were ordered to move from Texas territory up to Point Isabel at the mouth of the Rio Grande, an action clearly calculated to trigger war. This overt action produced the desired effect.

It was unlikely that Taylor's army would have drawn a Mexican attack had it remained in Texas, since Mexican forces had not entered that territory for several years. Mexico doubtless realized the inevitability of losing Texas. But the movement of Taylor's army to Point Isabel was different, a clear violation. The area between the Nueces River and the Great River had never been part of the Texas territory, nor had Texans ever lived there. The Nueces had long been regarded by Texans and Mexicans alike as the boundary between the two areas. Yet Polk maintained it was American soil because many Texans, with little reason, claimed the area. Thus the new aggression by Polk had no basis in regard to the Texas boundary. Rather it was a bold, illegal land grab based on America's sudden claim to the territory beyond the Nueces and up to the Rio Grande. Most Americans realized this claim was patently false. By moving American troops into an area which had always been considered part of Mexico, Polk hoped to precipitate a war and ultimately to gain the needed leverage to acquire New Mexico and California. Even had there been some possibility the area belonged to Texas, the movement of American troops into so controversial an area was clearly a signal that negotiations had ended and a challenge to war was being hurled at Mexico.

Polk waited impatiently in Washington for news of the outbreak of fighting so he could deliver his war message to Congress. Meanwhile General Taylor had indeed encountered the Mexican Army. But the first unfriendly exchanges consisted of written warnings, not bullets, and the Mexicans clearly had the best of this paper battle. They pointed out that they viewed the Americans' trespass on Mexican soil as an act of aggression. They further pointed out the aggressive implications of an army entering a territory currently under dispute between two nations. The Mexicans stated it appeared the Americans no longer were satisfied merely with Texas, but wanted to take a large part of Tamaulipas, the northeasternmost province of Mexico, as well. General Taylor, discomfited that the Mexicans might limit their attacks to paper, decided to take sterner measures. He ordered the blockade of the Rio Grande, thus cutting off supplies to the Mexican town of Matamoros, a provocative act of military aggression.

Meanwhile Polk proceeded with his plans for other parts of the continent. In California, a band of American settlers captured the town of Sonoma and hoisted the Bear Flag over it. Captain John C. Fremont entered the state in charge of a sixty-two man United States "surveying" party. The Mexican officials, suspicious because all Fremont's men were well-armed, ordered them out of the province. Fremont, under secret orders from President Polk to be on hand in the event of outbreak of war with Mexico, refused to leave California. Instead, he and his small army fortified a position atop a mountain peak and raised the American flag. Since the territory was Mexican and war had not been declared, this act was a gross provocation. It made clear that the Americans desired California and intended to annex it. Nonetheless, Fremont soon thought better of his indiscretion, hauled down Old Glory, and marched off with his troops to the aid of the Sonoma rebels. Nor did the U.S. warships lying off the California coast add to Mexican-American good-will. Polk then sent a spy on a mission through Mexico, bearing a secret message for the American consul in Monterey, California. Polk instructed the consul to actively cultivate an attitude in California favorable to the transfer of the territory to the United States.

Meanwhile, in Washington, Polk could not wait. An impulsive man, he would have preferred an attack by Mexico, but since it was slow in coming, he decided to proceed. With this in mind, he drafted a war message for Congress. The reasons he cited to justify the declaration of war were of the weakest variety. Mexico he said, had failed to pay its debts to several American citizens, and the Mexican government had refused to officially receive the U.S. minister in Mexico City. With his cabinet in full accord, Polk prepared to send his message to Congress.

As fate would have it, a dispatch from General Taylor arrived that night, relating that a small contingent of Taylor's troops had been attacked in the region between the Nueces and the Rio Grande, and that several Americans had been killed. Taylor had finally succeeded in provoking an attack. Congress, unaware of the extent to which Taylor and his army had pressured the Mexicans, was swept with anger upon hearing of the American deaths. Although there was a strong dissenting vote, war was declared. Just as, in 1812, there had been a large number of legislators who refused to commit America to a needless war against a nation which posed no threat, so there were many in Congress opposed to war with Mexico. Moreover, unlike 1812, the alleged foe had not impressed American sailors nor blockaded American ships. Mexico's sole offense was that of trying to retain territories which her avaricious northern neighbor desired. This was clear to many U.S. leaders. Congressman Abraham Lincoln spoke out vehemently against the war, even challenging the veracity of Polk's war address. He challenged the President to name one spot of American soil in Texas where a single drop of American blood had been shed.

Meanwhile warships anchored off California landed U.S. troops there as soon as word arrived of the declaration of war. Colonel Stephen W. Kearny was ordered to march down the Santa Fe Trail, recruiting an "army of the West" as he went, to take possession of New Mexico, and thereafter, California. Kearny's mission succeeded. His forces took Santa Fe and Los Angeles. Thereafter, he served as military governor of California until May, 1847.

Though the initial U.S. invasion of New Mexico and California was completed peacefully, insurgents in both areas soon rebelled against the occupying American forces. At Los Angeles a band of insurgents captured the American garrison and then went on to win several battles. They were finally subdued six months later. By the end of the War with Mexico, the American Army held precarious control again of New Mexico and California. The vast land area of California presented some problems to the American invaders, as did the confusion over who actually was in charge of the invasion forces. However, invasion and conquest of the territories was accomplished with relative ease, so weak were the Mexican forces garrisoned there.

In the interim American forces in Texas rallied and marched into Mexico, heading toward the capital. The Mexican army, large but poorly trained and even more poorly equipped, had more officers than fighting men. Conversely, the well-supplied American army was led by a host of eager young West Point graduates out to win their reputations. The war was well managed by the Americans, except at the highest level—President Polk. Winfield Scott and Zachary Taylor, though performing excellently as generals, were of a different political persuasion than Polk, who feared their growing popularity with the American people. For this reason, he sought to appoint a politically inert general to take charge of the American forces. Congress, fortunately, did not approve this purely partisan scheme, recognizing that General Scott was a most able leader. Polk, who had blatantly placed party politics above the interests of his country, was overruled. Under Scott, the war with Mexico was won without the loss of a single battle. Nonetheless one fight particularly stirred Mexican pride. At Chapultepec, near Mexico City, a group of young Mexican boys from a military academy fought valiantly against the American forces. The boys refused to retreat. None was ever to return home again.

The fight to conquer Mexico proved bloody, the defenders putting up strong resistance. Yet the war was an uneven conquest, won by an army that never numbered more than 10,000 Americans. Mexican resistance was fired by the return of the exiled Santa Anna. Ironically, President Polk had arranged for his release in the belief that Santa Anna would work for peace on American terms, but the fiery old Mexican was staunchly anti-American and rallied his countrymen to repel the invaders.

The Treaty of Guadalupe Hidalgo ratified by the U.S. Senate in March, 1848 ended the war, and Mexico was stripped of half her land holdings. The treaty acquired for the United States not only Texas, but a land area one and one-half times the size of the Louisiana Purchase, and increased the total size of the United States by one-third. The U.S. paid Mexico approximately $18,500,000 for the new area. Some 13,000 American lives were lost in the war.

The triumph in the name of Manifest Destiny was a bitter

loss to dismembered Mexico. Resentment there was fanned not only by the huge loss of territory, but by the American notion of Manifest Destiny as well. Bitterness spread throughout Latin America. In contrast many Americans proclaimed at the time that the Mexicans should be grateful for losing only half their country, and many American expansionists were angry that the U.S. did not take all of Mexico. In 1848 the United States had a mission, a "call" from God, to demonstrate the success of democracy, the inalienable rights of free men to spread it over the earth. Americans were willing to foment revolution and personally assist it, to begin war, spill blood, and wrest away half the territories of weaker powers—all in the name of Manifest Destiny.

CHAPTER V

Civil War: Democracy Fails

The outbreak of the American Civil War signified the failure of three national phenomena: the Constitution, the federal government, and the democratic process. A large segment of the nation refused to abide by the results of the national election of 1860 and expressed unwillingness to continue as a part of the United States. America's democratic government proved unsuccessful in its efforts to peacefully resolve internal conflict and reunite the North and South. Americans turned their backs on representative government, resorting to violence and killing in the effort to resolve sectional differences. This was America's darkest hour.

Over 600,000 men died in the Civil War, making it the world's costliest, most destructive event in terms of lives and property during America's history. The aftermath reaffirmed that North and South were one nation, but it had done so through war, rather than through the democratic institutions America's founding fathers had prized so highly. The Reconstruction period that ensued perpetuated the sectional animosities that originally had led to civil war and which continue to divide America. The Revisionist school of historians view the civil war as a needless and tragic event which could have been averted had the leaders of North and South acted as statesmen rather than fanatics.

The Civil War was ignited by numerous factors, including Southern slavery, the economic and political domination of the North, the agrarian position of the South, and cultural differences between the sections. But none of these differences justified war. This "repressible" conflict erupted as a result of folly, stupidity and arrogance on both sides. Southerners aligned against the North as they were increasingly pressured by the abolitionists. The charges of "immorality" that Northerners hurled against Southern slave-owners enraged the latter, who viewed themselves as decent, responsible men, for the majority treated their slaves well and provided them with security. For Southerners, this treatment of the blacks justified their role in enforcing servitude. Few even considered the question of the black man's right to freedom.

The Civil War was especially needless and unfortunate because without it slavery doubtless would have died of natural causes within several decades. Historians' estimates place the date of hypothetical "natural" emancipation without war as early as 1870. This is borne out by several historic factors: few Southern plantations were operating profitably in 1864, and those that were showed only marginal gains even in the best years. The cost of slaves was high, yet usually they did not work hard and thus were often a liability. Many slaves handled tools and farm machinery carelessly, often causing breakage or loss, and thus compounding their costliness. Slavery also retarded the economy of the South by tying up capital that was sorely needed to develop manufacturing. As Southern industry grew, slavery declined because it was an impractical source of labor for this segment of the economy. As a result of these and other factors, the number of Southern slaveowners was steadily declining from the minority of Southerners who formerly had owned slaves. Few had large numbers of slaves. Before the War, Abraham Lincoln believed the slaves could be freed by the federal government's purchasing them from their Southern owners, a plan called "compensated emancipation." Had war been averted this plan undoubtedly would have been effected.

Slavery had also reached its geographical limits in America's westward expansion because of agricultural factors in the Southwest, chiefly the absence of cotton crops in this and other areas. There were also other factors portending a foreseeable end to slavery. Many countries, such as Britain and France, had already abolished slavery, and a worldwide abolition movement was gaining momentum. Religious leaders were beginning to emphasize the incompatibility of the age-old institution with the emerging concept of the natural rights of men, and political and economic leaders the inherent unproductivity of the system. Opposition to the slave trade was soon written into international law. Many nations freed their slaves gradually by declaring their children "free" when they attained the age of eighteen. All of this supports the contention that had America's bloody Civil War not been fought the nation's slaves nonetheless would have been freed. Such a planned emancipation doubtless would have achieved speedier integration of the blacks into a predominantly white American society.

The second-cited cause of the Civil War, sectional rivalry, is also baseless and insufficient. Secession of the South from the Union had been successfully averted in 1851, a decade earlier, by a series of compromises; one may ask why it was not similarly averted in 1861. The answer lies in the passionate growing hatred of the South for the North and vice versa, rather than in any truly irreconcilable differences between their respective philosophies or goals. The threat to Southern power implicit in the events of the expanding Republic prior to 1850 actually was far greater than any threat posed by Lincoln's election. In 1850, for example, California was admitted to the Union as a free state, destroying the traditional Southern balance of power in the Senate, an outcome potentially more ominous for the South than the election of a moderate Republican a decade later. The first threat of Southern secession occurred in 1851, when South Carolina, represented by John Calhoun, threatened to secede from the Union unless the North agreed to every Southern demand. Yet on these issues the North and South both made compromises, engineered by Henry Clay. Secession was prevented and war averted. One can only speculate whether, 10 years, later, statesmanship comparable to Clay's could not have averted the disaster of 1861. The growing sectional rift might also have been effectively resolved in this decade had not the nation been led by weak Presidents, incapable of calming the sectional rivalries and working for a meaningful integration of interests.

One reason the North-South conflict was more intense in 1861 than 10 years earlier was that, throughout this decade, incompetent politicians in both North and South had continuously fanned the flames of hatred. By hurling accusations at the rival section, state and local politicians could both divert voter attention from the controversial issues within their constituencies and win the support of a growing fanatic element. These politicians contrived fictitious issues between North and South to seize support and gain votes, knowing most voters would not be offended by blanket condemnation of other sections. Over the years this irresponsible growing agitation heightened sectional resentments and, ultimately, public rage. The emotional turbulence wrought by these self-seeking politicians helped plunge North and South into Civil War.

In 1861, as a result of this political warmongering, Lincoln's election precipitated a reaction of panic in the South wholly disproportionate to the event. Southern leaders, prodded by powerful passions, reacted irrationally. Lincoln was not a wild-eyed abolitionist intent on crushing the South. Rather he was a moderate who, like statesmen North and South, believed in the eventual demise of slavery, but who posed no ominous threat to the South. Nor did Southerners believe Lincoln would take radical action; he eschewed immediate uncompensated liberation of the slaves and openly admitted he did not know how their liberation could be achieved and the emancipated slaves absorbed successfully into the economy. Lincoln believed that Negroes were inferior to whites. Thus, on his election, the rational course would have been for the Southern states to adopt a "wait-and-see" policy. Lincoln had demonstrated no great qualities prior to his election, had produced no outstanding record of achievement, and Southerners might therefore have logically surmised that he would not take precipitous action against slavery. Instead, rashly, the Southern states seceded, one after another, before Lincoln was inaugurated.

At the time, the political power of the South in Congress was still a viable force. In fact, in 1861 the Democrats had a majority in both houses of Congress as well as a very strong position in the Supreme Court. By their withdrawal, the Southern states lost all hope of achieving what they had been seeking for decades: a portion of the federal territories and enforcement of the fugitive slave laws. Through their rash, improvident action they undermined all possibility that America's new territories could become slave states and simultaneously ensured that, thenceforth, any escaped slave would never be returned. For the South, it had been an adolescent act, striking out against the North no matter how badly its own interests were hurt. The South, irresponsibly refusing to abide by the election of Lincoln, seceded even before putting the move to its citizens for a vote, a measure sorely warranted in such a major action.

In the early days of 1861, the nation needed a strong leader more than it ever had before, a leader who could calm the rampant fears of North and South, yet act with courage, strength, and foresight. His major task would be to persuade North and South to calmly evaluate the facts, and then, effect compromise. No such leader existed. President Buchanan had equivocated and bumbled. Even worse, Lincoln, the President-elect who would prove himself an able leader only a few months later, did nothing in this initial period except grow a beard. Though not yet inaugurated, President-elect Lincoln should have taken affirmative action in these four months of crisis, if only to reduce the South's traumatic reaction to his election. He should have clearly disavowed to the South all implications of his immediate abolition of slavery, for he had no plans to do so. Instead of fretting in Illinois over appointments to his Cabinet, he should have met with Southern leaders and laid an early groundwork for sectional reconciliation. Such effects warranted in this time of national emergency were clearly beyond Buchanan's abilities, but Lincoln might have veered the tide had he tried. Compounding the crisis was a last-minute attempt to stave off secession called "Crittenden's Compromise," a compromise plan which proposed extending the "slave line" (latitude 36° 30′) to the Pacific. Though several similar compromises had been discussed among federal officials, Crittenden's merited the most serious consideration. Lincoln, however, rejected this proposed compromise out of hand, and replaced it with no alternative of his own, apparently believing the South's threat of secession a mere bluff. This man who rejected Crittenden's Compromise was the same Lincoln who years later said if saving the Union required not freeing a single slave, he would be willing to do so.

Lincoln's primary Presidential opponent, Stephen Douglas, of the Lincoln-Douglas debate fame, rose above personal ambition after his defeat and traveled throughout the Union denouncing secession. Douglas even went into the deep South, pleading with voters there to abide by the election of Lincoln. Threats, snubs, and well-aimed eggs all failed to deter Douglas, whose earnest cause was that of saving the Union. It was Lincoln who should have taken this deliberate action when the first Southern state seceded, denouncing secession and working behind the scenes with Southern leaders toward sectional reconciliation.

Secretary of State William Seward recommended to Lincoln that a war be incited with a foreign power, thus reuniting the sympathies and energies of North and South in a common national cause. Lincoln rejected outright this unscrupulous proposal. Only a month after Lincoln assumed office, the first shots were fired at Fort Sumter.

By the day of Lincoln's inaugural the South had seized vast areas of federal property within their states. Lincoln assured the rebellious Southerners he did not plan to send Northerners into their area to reclaim federal property. His action suggested he wanted to buy time to devise strategy for bringing the seceded states back into the Union. Fort Sumter was at the time one of the few federal properties in the South that still remained in government hands. All of Lincoln's Cabinet members advised against reinforcing Sumter because of the potential repercussions such a move might have. In fact, Secretary of State Seward went so far as to promise Southern representatives that federal troops soon would be withdrawn. Though Lincoln was unaware of this promise, the South naturally assumed it had his approval. Thus the government's continuing retention and ultimate reprovisioning of Fort Sumter was viewed by Southern leaders as a gross breach of promise on Lincoln's part. Meanwhile, underestimating all likelihood of the terrible blood-bath that was to ensue, Lincoln decided force was the only means to dissuade the South from a prolonged period of secession.

Major Robert Anderson, the commander of Fort Sumter, was negotiating with the Governor of South Carolina the possible surrender of the fort, yet he refused to surrender while the flow of provisions continued from the North. Lincoln decided to send a ship laden with supplies to Fort Sumter. South Carolina viewed this as a hostile act. Lincoln and other Northern leaders knew that, if fighting broke out, Virginia, the largest and most powerful state in the South, would secede from the Union. Were this to occur, it would add a powerful member to the alliance of seceding states and deal a damaging blow to the Union cause. Thus, for the North, it was vital no sectional fighting erupt before peaceful negotiations begin between Lincoln and Southern leaders toward achieving a compromise.

Lincoln knew Fort Sumter had no strategic military importance, but he apparently held little hope for a peaceful settlement with the South and decided against buying time to effect a compromise. He dispatched a courier to the Governor of South Carolina to announce his intentions. The act was comparable to waving a red flag in front of a bull. Before the federal supply ship arrived, South Carolinian troops opened fire on Fort Sumter and the fort was forced to surrender.

Neither North nor South were well organized, but the outbreak of fighting at Fort Sumter served both sides well. An immediate surge of spirited voluntary enlistment ensued in both camps. Virginia seceded, as did other Southern states. Apparently still regarding the rebellion as a limited insurrection, Lincoln called up only 75,000 volunteers. Four-million men ultimately would fight in the four-year conflict. Of the host of factors which had served to split a great nation into warring factions, the clear lack of foresight and statesmanship among the national leaders of the preceding decade was perhaps the central cause. Still another was Lincoln's failure to work for a satisfactory compromise between North and South because of his belief that neither secession nor war would occur.

The Civil War was long and bloody. Though the South would probably have fared better had the war occurred in 1851, it still possessed several advantages: it had great hopes of foreign intervention or military support in its behalf; it had better military leadership and better morale; and it was fighting a defensive war. The possibility of European nations intervening on behalf of the Confederacy loomed large, because they would benefit were the powerful United States divided into two smaller, less powerful nations.

Lincoln offered Robert E. Lee the position of commander-in-chief of the Union Army, recognizing the outstanding tactical military skills of the Virginian. Lee was torn between his loyalties to the Union and to his family, friends and native Southern state. In the end, Lee's allegiance to Virginia proved stronger; he soon accepted the role at the helm of the Southern Army. This was a costly loss for the North, for Lee ultimately proved to be the Civil War's most outstanding military leader, his performance truly brilliant. It is ironic that though Lee opposed slavery and had freed his own blacks, he led the cause of the people that many believed were solely advocating their right to maintain the immoral institution.

The North had several strategic advantages: superior industrial production and output; greater population; better railroads; and superior Naval power, assuring control of the Atlantic shores. Despite these Northern advantages, however, there remained several possibilities which could have contributed to a Southern victory: intervention by France or Britain on the side of the Confederacy; failure or refusal of Northerners to respond to the conscription and production needs of the Union; and, finally, the continued inability of the North to find an effective military commander.

The odds against the South appeared staggering. The North had 21,000,000 people, compared to only 5,500,000 whites in the South. The North's economic capacity to wage war was even more preponderant, about seven times as great as that of the Confederacy. Yet other factors served to equalize the conflict.

86

Lincoln chose indecisive, often bungling generals who led the first two years of the war, not coming upon Ulysses S. Grant until the third year. In battle after battle during the early months of fighting the Union forces were defeated by Southern forces of equal or lesser size. Lee carefully sized up each Northern general and devised his respective strategies accordingly. It is clear that superior military leadership made the real difference in the early battles of the Civil War.

The North's slow mobilization of its economic resources was largely due to inefficiencies in Lincoln's administration. He failed to muster an efficient team of advisors and did not implement a central agency to coordinate the varied departments of government. The faction-ridden Cabinet that surrounded him provided no help in the critical wartime coordination of resources and production, and Lincoln controlled neither his Cabinet nor Congress with the firmness essential to the task.

In the first major battle of the Civil War, at Bull Run, the green Union troops were badly routed. The Union troops were driven back by the enemy and quickly fled, dropping their arms and racing through the ranks of foolish sightseers who had traveled from Washington to watch the engagement. The Northerners fled to the fortifications ringing the Capitol city. Though this early disgrace was not to be often repeated by the Union forces, their lack of military leadership early in the war led to a series of poor Northern showings. Lincoln's first choice, General George B. McClellan, proved to be an indecisive man who moved his armies slowly and cautiously, and was clearly no match for Lee. The President eventually placed McClellan under the command of General Halleck. At one point he allowed newly-appointed Halleck to pull back advancing Northern armies. To have allowed this retreat was probably Lincoln's worst military blunder, for it probably cost the North early victory in the war. Once again McClellan was placed in command and once again replaced after more costly errors. After McClellan, Lincoln appointed one general after another: Burnside, Hooker, Meade and finally Grant.

Because the Union Army was plagued by a lack of volunteer manpower after the initial rush of enlistees at the inception of the fighting, the North was forced to pass a Conscription Act which soon triggered bloody draft riots in New York and other areas. Dissenters against the war were numerous and often vociferous in both North and South. Eventually, the tide of war turned in favor of the North; Lincoln found outstanding generals in Grant, Sherman, and Sheridan. This, plus the greater population and industrial capacity of the North, assured her victory.

The events of those grim war years have been widely chronicled, but several lesser-known incidents warrant examination. One was the Trent Affair, a minor disagreement between the Union and England which served to repeat the pattern of the War of 1812, but in reverse. It will be recalled that a major factor inciting the War of 1812 was America's protest against the impressment by the British Navy of sailors off American boats. Similarly, in 1861, a Union warship halted a British vessel, the mailcarrier *Trent*, and forcibly arrested two Confederate representatives enroute to England. This was a violation of international law similar to those perpetrated by England prior to 1812, since Britain, in 1861, was a neutral country. Since the *Trent* carried neither arms nor soldiers the Union had no right under international law to halt her or seize her passengers. Lincoln disavowed the act and released the imprisoned Confederates. His action was not motivated as much by regard for international law as by fear of losing the sympathy of the British people, or worse, precipitating war with Britain. Fortunately for the Union Lincoln's apology and release of the prisoners soothed British indignation and the event passed without further incident.

Lincoln's preoccupation with winning the favor of major European powers moved him to further acts. In 1862 he issued the famed Emancipation Proclamation, calculated to win foreign support and end the possibility that Britain or France might intervene on the side of the Confederacy. Thus the primary aim of the Proclamation was not to free Southern slaves but to gain the favor of the British. Once the French and British perceived the Civil War as a moral and humanitarian quest—to free the slaves—rather than a mere nationalistic battle to preserve the Union of states, their sentiments swung quickly to the North. The Proclamation was also aimed at bolstering Northern morale and generating patriotic fervor in order to spur flagging Union Army enlistments. Ironically, at the onset of the war between the States, only a handful of Northerners had wanted to fight to free the slaves, but as the war dragged on the risks and sacrifices of life and limb required greater justification: the slaves must be freed. After all, it had been the issue of slavery that incited this raging war. By making the War's primary goal the emancipation of the slaves, Lincoln succeeded in sparking Northern spirits. He knew that issuance of the Proclamation would spur many Southern slaves to revolt or run away and join the Union Army, though this was a lesser consideration. The Emancipation Proclamation thus was chiefly a strategic diplomatic and military maneuver.

In itself the Proclamation did not emancipate a single slave. Those slaves that would ultimately be freed lived in areas that would be conquered by the Union Army. Nor did the Proclamation apply to slaves in Southern regions already held by federal troops or to slaves in the border states. A London newspaper observed sarcastically, "The principle is not that a human being cannot justly own another, but that he cannot own him unless he is loyal to the United States."

For America's slaves, as this criticism noted, the Emancipation Proclamation was but an extremely limited enlargement of civil rights. Further, the Proclamation was unconstitutional since slavery was set forth as legal in the laws of fifteen states and as an issue wholly under state jurisdiction. Lincoln, however, moved to justify the Proclamation by declaring it a wartime necessity. Surprisingly then, two years later, that the President refused to sign a bill presented by Congress that would officially abolish slavery, stating he believed it to be "unconstitutional." Lincoln explained the contradiction implicit in this action by saying that measures of questionable Constitutionality may be taken in wartime, but could not be allowed in peacetime. Only the ultimate ratification of the Thirteenth Amendment to the Constitution achieved the freeing of slaves in America, a feat usually attributed in error to Lincoln's Emancipation Proclamation.

Lincoln's wartime disregard of the Constitution has already been mentioned. During the war years he often ignored this venerable document he staunchly purported to defend, repeatedly citing "wartime powers" as his justification. In one such action, he suspended the Constitutional writ of *habeas corpus*, an American citizen's right, upon arrest, to be brought before a court to fairly determine the justice of his imprisonment. As a result in ensuing months over 13,000 persons were arrested and unjustly confined. In another supra-Constitutional action Lincoln approved the admission of West Virginia, a section of the State of Virginia, into the Union without the prior approval of the state or the majority of its citizenry, although the Constitution specifically declares a state cannot be divided without its consent. Virginia's legislature refused to give such consent and its electorate was never queried.

Further Presidential acts of questionable Constitutionality involved the imprisonment of civilians by the Union Army. In such cases military officers charged specific civilians with disloyalty to the Union, imprisoned them and held them without trial. Still other citizens were arrested and tried in military courts, even in areas not under martial law. The Supreme Court finally ruled that civilians could not be tried in areas where civil courts were operative and the practice thereafter was discontinued.

Another supra-Constitutional liberty taken by Lincoln was the adoption and enforcement of America's first federal tax levy on personal income, a measure designed to raise funds to fortify Union forces. Income taxation did not, in fact, become legal until 1913, when a new Constitutional Amendment at last empowered the federal government to enforce such a levy.

Such measures were perhaps necessary; yet it remains ironic that Lincoln overrode Constitutional principles in time of war but was unwilling to negotiate comparatively simpler compromises prior to the four-year conflict that might well have prevented it. A result of Lincoln's transgressions upon the supreme law of the land was the ensuing thirty-five year reaction of Congress which thereafter dominated the Presidency with stern severity until Theodore Roosevelt assumed the helm of government at the turn of the century.

Eventually, under the pressure of Grant's aggressive strategies and the unending wave of Northern troops, weapons and supplies, the Confederacy began to falter. Its foreseeable defeat was hastened by widespread desertion in the ranks, crumbling morale, and the eventual destruction of its cities.

When the darkest hour in America's history ended and domestic bloodletting ceased, the nation was forced to face the unenviable task of rebuilding. This entailed not only the reconstruction of cities and towns, buildings and rail lines, but also the rebuilding of whole social, economic and political sectors of the republic.

Lincoln knew this would be a sensitive task. During the four years of civil war he had developed into a remarkable statesman, a truly great diplomatic figure. He realized the importance of drawing with compassion and charity the South back into the Union of states. He realized that malice toward the South at this juncture would injure the entire nation by perpetuating sectional ill-will and retarding the urgently needed move toward reconstruction. With Union victory assured he was careful to avoid the overtones of vindictiveness which characteristically accompany conquest and instead urged North and South toward tolerance, mercy, and reconstruction. The plan of Reconstruction proposed by Lincoln embodied policies most lenient toward the South. Viewed in retrospect his plan may have calmed sectional rivalries, but it is doubtful if even Lincoln could have achieved integration of blacks into American life.

After Lincoln's death Congress directed the Reconstruction process and its strict, if not harsh, policies heightened sectional hostilities, increased racial tensions and spurred ardent support for the opposition Democratic Party throughout the South, paving the way for the one-party system that largely has held sway there to this day. Though Congress enacted several needed reforms in the area of black civil rights, they nowhere approached the far-reaching restructuring of Southern institutions which would have established a real basis for equality of blacks. The South's major economic problem was that of transforming its largely agrarian society into a productive industrial economy, thus stimulating employment, income and land usage. Its key political problem was that of resuming its former role within the Constitutional framework of the Union. Its foremost social problem was that of integrating the liberated black into a predominantly white American society, educating him, and securing and ensuring his equal rights. These goals were in part incompatible with one another. In the years that followed they were fulfilled only in the most limited sense, and to this day they still have not been wholly accomplished. Lincoln was perhaps the one leader who could have started the nation on the path toward the needed comprehensive reconstruction, but even he might have failed, for the first indications of Congressional opposition to his plan surfaced even before his assassination.

After Lincoln's death there was little hope for his Reconstruction program. The weak Andrew Johnson quickly lost control of the nation to such Congressional leaders as Thad Stevens and Charles Sumner, both of whom thought the South should be punished for its secession and subsequent role in the War. These Republican leaders were also motivated by the desire to keep Southern Democrats out of Congress, thereby ensuring the preservation of their own power.

Rather than implementing Lincoln's plan, Congress decided on a harsher policy, sweeping away the South's individual state governments and sectioning it into five military districts, each controlled by a U.S. Army general. Southern leaders were responsible at least in part for the increasingly harsh measures imposed upon them because they had failed to accept the provisions of even the mild reconstruction formerly offered them. They had flatly resisted making concessions which in fact were not unreasonable. In one such instance they refused to enfranchise the liberated black, refused to adopt new state Constitutions guaranteeing blacks minimum civil rights, and refused to bar certain ex-Confederates from seeking official office, as demanded by the North. The two requirements regarding blacks could understandably be imposed upon the South, which, after all, had lost the war. But the requirement barring certain ex-Confederates office was harsh, since those proscribed comprised most of the South's former leadership.

Illogical arguments regarding the status of the South raged in both sections. The South, which earlier had seceded from the Union, declared after the Civil War that it was still in the Union. This was illogical since the South had long contended secession was legal. Equally illogical was the stand of the North. Though it had long contended that secession was illegal—in fact, impossible—after the Civil War the North maintained the seceded Southern states were not a part of the Union until they were formally readmitted. These ill-founded arguments hampered the cause of reunity.

During the late 1860's and into the 70's many blacks were elected to office in the South, men who had been slaves only a few years earlier. On the whole they fulfilled their offices competently and showed little vindictiveness toward their white constituents. One indication of this was their tendency to favor full rights for former Confederates almost without restriction. Also in Southern governments were a sprinkling of Northern "carpetbaggers" and Southern "scalawags," some of whom operated chiefly for personal gain, but many others of whom genuinely served the public interest. Unfortunately several Southern state governments were riddled with corruption at this time, but this proved to be more than merely a problem of the Southern states. All levels of government, municipal, county, state, and federal, including Grant's cabinet, were rife with unscrupulous politicians. Graft and self-interest dictated many phases of national policy.

As resentment grew throughout the South against Northern domination, the status of blacks declined. The number of blacks in public office diminished. They began to lose both their rights and the vote. Interest in the plight of the black was waning in the North. Soon he was left to fend for himself.

In 1868, a post-Civil War secret society of whites named the Ku Klux Klan launched a campaign to intimidate blacks, to deny them office, and to prevent them from voting by threat and harassment. The Klan lacked effective strength and size, but Southern leaders were becoming disaffected with the federal Reconstruction program. When these leaders openly began to oppose Reconstruction, the Southern intimidation of blacks became open and even "rightful."

Northern indifference stemmed from one major factor: most Northerners, like their Southern counterparts, were prejudiced against blacks. Once assured Southern blacks had been freed and would not be re-enslaved, the Northerners, their moral consciences salved, had no further interest in black welfare. Even the South's eventual defranchisement of the black right to vote by such means as poll taxes, property requirements, or prohibitive literacy tests failed to draw Northern opposition.

During the post-war years the U.S. Senate greatly enlarged its powers at the expense of the Executive and Judicial branches. This domination over the Presidency continued through the Reconstruction period until Theodore Roosevelt assumed the office at the turn of the century. While, during these years, the Senate virtually controlled the course of government, the House of Representatives, an inefficient and disorderly body at the time, barely was able to conduct its own business. For example, in 1878 the House could not pass on a vital appropriations bill because the members of an important House committee all were too drunk to prepare it. At the Capitol President Hayes, waiting with his entire Cabinet to sign the bill, fumed with indignation. After twelve long hours the representatives at last sobered sufficiently to complete the bill, and Hayes signed it.

From 1865 to 1900 the succession of U.S. Presidents registered weak, unimpressive performances: all stood in the dominant shadows of the U.S. Senate. Most were barely competent to serve at the top rung of government. Johnson was nearly impeached. Grant was a weak President whose administration was riddled with corruption. Despite his illustrious earlier military career he ranks as one of the least effectual Presidents. The nation compounded its error by re-electing him. Following Grant was Hayes, who hated to make decisions and was content to let Congress direct the country. Next was Garfield, who, in the four months he served before his assassination, proved an ineffectual leader. The four Presidents who followed him were equally inept and indecisive. In all, the eight successors to the Presidency after Lincoln recorded only mediocre performances. Their powerlessness in part resulted from reaction in Congress against the tremendous powers Lincoln had wielded and the unusual, often supra-Constitutional liberties he had used to achieve them.

The Presidential election of 1876 marked the climax of the Reconstruction period. This election was the nadir of America's democratic process; Rutherford Hayes was elevated to office amidst widespread cheating at the polls and corrupt political bargains. Hayes's opponent for office, J. Tilden, actually won both the electoral and popular votes. The Republicans were prepared to quickly reverse this defeat into victory by invalidating Southern votes. They telegraphed Republican Party aides in three states to invalidate all Democratic ballots and the revised returns thereby showed Hayes the winner. Thirteen-thousand Democratic ballots were invalidated in Louisiana alone. The switch in the electoral votes of the three states gave Hayes the needed electoral count to win, though not a popular majority. Protesting this outrage, the Democrats filed their own returns with Congress. Neither party was willing to concede.

After great wrangling and confusion an Electoral Commission was appointed to determine the true winner. It was then revealed that Democrats had forcibly prevented thousands of Southern Negroes from voting, a transgression that perhaps was equal in effect to the Republicans' vote-invalidation. The Governor of Louisiana offered to sell his state's electoral votes to either candidate for several hundred thousand dollars, and the Florida election board offered to sell its state's electoral votes for the same price. The federal Electoral Commission, assigned to objectively determine the winning contender, did so in a purely partisan manner without regard to the electorate. Every Commission member without exception voted for the candidate of his party. When Rutherford Hayes won, the Democrats were ready to fight the decision, but those Democrats in power were willing to accept Hayes as President in return for political concessions. In exchange for their concession to his questionable "election," Hayes agreed that, once in office, he would withdraw all federal troops from the South. He also made several other "agreements." The electoral votes again were counted, and Hayes was officially declared the winner, the vote tallying 185 to 184!

Thus, the Reconstruction period came to an end with a contest reflecting the worst mockery of free democratic election in America's history. Corruption was rife, the President was an impotent figurehead, and sectional rivalry continued as did the serious problems surrounding the acceptance and integration of the emancipated blacks. Instead of dealing with these issues, however, Republican candidates gained votes in the North by emphasizing the terrible bloodshed which the South and, by association, the Democratic Party, had caused in years past. In heated resentment Southerners unthinkingly voted the straight Democratic ticket, regardless of issues or candidates. Though Reconstruction presented an opportunity to resolve many of the nation's pre-war sectional differences, the reforms that were effected were limited. The "healing" Reconstruction years only intensified the nation's ills.

By the end of Reconstruction the United States was emerging as a vast young power with all of the wealth and woes inherent in that distinction. There rose to prominence a class of plutocrats motivated by the "Gospel of Wealth," and even the poor dreamed of someday joining their ranks. The Industrial Age was well underway, and gross national product soared. Living conditions of the laboring class were both better and worse than before as thousands poured into the nation's cities. Cities grew rapidly, and urban problems multiplied: inadequate sewage systems, poor transportation and developing slums became critical issues. Industrial waste and urban pollution transformed rivers and lakes into open sewers. Overcrowding and inadequate housing contributed to urban unrest.

Prior to the industrial age America had been a predominantly rural society. Those who were employed on farms and ranches or owned small farms had food and shelter even during periods of economic depression. But the depths of the industrial cycle had in depression years an inevitably harsh impact on urban families who relied directly on the economy even for their food. The unemployed could not obtain food in the city as they had on the farm, and for shelter they were doomed to the most sub-standard slum housing. Disease and crime flourished in these slum areas. The dual standard which the nation fostered during the age of industrialization in the late 1800's led to this period being called the "Gilded Age," because beneath the glitter of vast wealth for the fortunate few were grim and insoluble problems for the many—problems which the captains of industry chose to ignore.

Until the advent of the progressive era of Teddy Roosevelt capitalism, untouched by government intervention except that which benefited big business, generated inherent far-reaching problems which did not prove self-correcting. Cyclical depressions every few years transformed the working masses into the jobless poor. Nor did labor share in private industry's prosperity to the extent that it contributed to it. The wealthy eschewed other worthwhile goals in the greedy pursuit of material goods. Capitalism bred these and other ills until, in time, it was realized only government intervention or control could correct or restrain them. For America, unguided capitalism was, at best, a mixed blessing.

CHAPTER VI

Dispossession of the American Indian

Within two centuries after the arrival of the first European colonists the entire American territory had been wrested away from its former long-time inhabitants, the American Indians. This gross dispossession of a whole ethnic society, largely achieved by murderous massacres, land-grabs, economic pressures, and deceptive legislation, looms in the annals of American history as an unprecedented and unpardonable deed of aggression. The rapid conquest of the outnumbered Indians was a bloody one. More significantly, it crushed the New World's native culture. In this the conquest was far more devastating than the military victories and territorial occupation achieved in the lands conquered by Ghengis Khan and Napoleon. These earlier conquerors left the vanquished peoples and their cultures largely intact. But the settlers' conquest of the total land area of the United States delivered a death blow to Indian culture. Greatly reduced in number, helpless and confused, the Indian people were driven off their lands and confined to small reservations. Few remnants of their former lifestyles or culture remained, leading to the subsequent eradication of the Indian way of life.

The dispossession of the American Indian began with the arrival of the first European settlers to the New World. Armed with guns and eager to amass the legendary "riches" awaiting them in the new virgin territory, they confronted the native inhabitants with demands. The first of these were for pearls, slaves and gold. Next the settlers demanded that the Indians surrender their faiths and convert to the Christian religion.

Their final and most emphatic demand was for the Indian's lands.

Some Indians submitted meekly to these demands while others resisted them with ferocity. Still others fought the encroachments of the white man in "civilized ways"—through the courts and by appeals to the government. Hopelessly outnumbered militarily, the Indians looked to the whites' government for justice. In every instance the results were the same: the Indians lost all they had. The white man was far superior in guns and numbers, and he possessed perhaps the most potent weapon of all, the diseases he imported to the New World. The history of the Indian dispossession in America is a continuous cycle of invasion of Indian land, followed by relocation of the Indians to a smaller territory, after which greedy whites quickly invaded the smaller area, leading to a repetition of the cycle. The numbers of Indians soon decreased as rapidly as did their land. Though many were victims of starvation and murder, cholera and smallpox loomed as the biggest killers. Having no immunity to these diseases, the Indians succumbed by the thousands. So effective were these diseases in destroying whole tribes that a few whites seriously considered germ warfare as a means of conquest.

The earliest recorded act of aggression against the Indians occurred in Jamestown in 1607 when the first permanent English settlers moved onto the land of the Powhatan Indian tribe. Thereafter the colonists sorely mistreated the Powhatan and would have been driven out had it not been for the marriage of Pocahontas, the daughter of the powerful Powhatan chief, to settler John Rolfe. This marriage prevented the great chief from attacking the colonists. By the time of Pocahontas's death the white settlers had increased in sufficient number to seize the balance of power. In 1622 they attacked the Powhatans and drove them from their ancestral lands.

Invasion of Indian land continued in the Jamestown area until, a half century later, "King Philip's War" erupted. In proportion to population it was one of the deadliest wars in American history. Several tribes were almost totally annihilated. The Indian leader, King Philip, was also killed in battle, and the settlers displayed his head on a pole in Plymouth for the next twenty years. The outcome was disastrous for the Indians; the few survivors were sold into slavery in the West Indies. Today several tribes which participated in the war are extinct.

William Penn demonstrates how events might have been different. He purchased title to Indian lands rather than taking them forcefully. He also cultivated the friendship of the natives and saw to it that any disputes arising between the whites and the Indians were arbitrated in council. During these years, though the Indians waged relentless attacks on other colonies, not a single Quaker was injured and the Quakers coexisted peacefully with the Indians for sixty years.

After Penn's death the Pennsylvania colony continued to grow. Bereft of Penn's prudent leadership, the colonists soon pushed onto Indian land. The Indians sought to defend it and in the years to come were pushed further into the Ohio Valley. Like other Indian bands prior to the Revolution, they moved farther and farther West, forerunners of a wave of white settlers.

The Indians also figured significantly in America's early military actions. During the French and Indian War Indians of various tribes fought on both sides. Their cause suffered, with the defeat of the French, since French policies regarding the Indians characteristically were more benign than those of the American colonists. Indians also played a significant role in the American Revolution. The Oneida and Tuscarora tribes fed Washington's starving soldiers at Valley Forge, while the white settlers sold food and supplies to the British. Washington claimed that American independence could not have been gained without the help of the Indians.

After the Revolution, no longer hindered by the line of Demarcation the British had drawn earlier across the crest of the Appalachians, settlers swarmed westward across the mountains and into the wilderness. Settling into the rich valleys, they felled the dense trees and razed the underbrush, frightened off wild game that the neighboring Indians looked to for sustenance. The Indians' needs were ignored. Washington's benevolent attitude toward them caused a decline in his public popularity, since most whites believed the natives to be "heathens" or primitives who warranted little or no consideration. When Washington recommended that the Indians be paid for the lands usurped from them by the settlers, he was hung in effigy. Meanwhile the settlers pushed relentlessly onto Indian lands, and the frontier was immersed in bloody fighting. The Indians refused to submit. They were fighting not only for their land but for their way of life. In contrast, the whites were fighting for a few more acres of farmland.

Finally, in 1791, the young republic sent an army of 500 men into the wilderness to quell the Indian uprising. The army, led by General St. Clair, marched into Indian territory and soon was surrounded and crushed, suffering enormous casualties. Washington sought to make peace by talking to the Indians but the latter insisted that peace was possible only if the white usurpers stayed off their land.

In 1793 General "Mad" Anthony Wayne marched into Indian territory with 3,600 men to incite the Battle of Fallen Timbers, in which the Indians were defeated. Thereafter Wayne commanded his men to raze the Indian homes and cornfields, destroying their sources of food and shelter for the coming winter. The Indians thus were forced to cede 25,000 square miles to the United States. Many more such treaties were to be forced upon them by America's militias during the next 100 years as the Indians succumbed to defeat after crushing defeat in the nation's steady westward expansion.

Among those who notably mistreated the Indians was William Henry Harrison, who later was to become the ninth President of the United States. As territorial governor of the Indian lands he exerted continuous pressure on them to move farther westward. After invading whites marched on Indian lands and cleared the forests, Harrison bought the land from the distraught Indians for almost nothing. He would negotiate such land acquisitions with only several chiefs, when in fact the land was actually owned in common by many tribes. This impelled a powerful Shawnee Indian leader, Tecumseh, to strike out against Harrison and his dishonorable dealings, which over the years had wrested 33,000,000 acres of land from the hapless Indians. Tecumseh traveled from the Great Lakes to the Gulf of Mexico, preaching to his people the need for a great pan-Indian alliance to resist the white invasion. Meanwhile Harrison determined to attack the Indians before Tecumseh could return from the South. He marched on an Indian town at the head of a large army, ignoring a peace message dispatched by the Indians. The Indians, learning this message had not been acknowledged by Harrison, decided to attack first under the leadership of Tecumseh's brother, the Prophet. They were badly defeated in the battle of Tippecanoe. Tecumseh returned to learn of the Indian defeat and the dashing of his hopes for the great alliance. He fled to Canada, was made a General in the British Army, and died in battle against the Americans during the War of 1812. Harrison's victory over the Indians at Tippecanoe gained him a reputation for military leadership which ultimately led to his election to the Presidency.

America's treatment of the Delaware Indians also exemplifies the unending pressures exerted to continually push the Indians back in the face of advancing settlers. The Delawares, who called themselves the Lenapi ("the people"), were driven by Quaker colonials after Penn's death from Pennsylvania into the Ohio Valley, and there signed treaties of peace with the young federal government. In 1778 the U.S. guaranteed the Delawares all the territorial rights they had previously possessed; another treaty, several years later, sanctioned the Indians' right to punish whites who attempted to settle on their land. As before the white man's treaties proved to be worth less than the paper they were written on. White settlers and surveyors soon moved onto the land which had been guaranteed the Indians' exclusive territory "for all time." The United States government, rather than drive the invading whites off the Indian soil, asked the Indians to make concessions. After the Battle of Fallen Timbers, the Delawares were pushed even further west, and, in 1817, the federal government deemed it expedient to cancel Indian title to all lands in the State of Ohio, although these had been guaranteed them by previous U.S. treaties. Today the majority of the remaining Delaware live in Oklahoma, far from the lands promised them two centuries earlier by the United States government.

The Cherokee Indians centered in Tennessee and Georgia presented a more stubborn obstacle to the white man's advance, but ultimately were brutally driven from their lands and relocated to a reservation in Oklahoma. The Cherokee continued to fight the whites, not militarily, but by becoming "civilized" and defending their rights in court. Their advancement over the course of a few years was brilliant and their case was won in the Supreme Court. But still white greed prevailed.

The Cherokee, a mountain people, were the largest tribe in the southwestern United States. Prior to the white advance they had been warlike and adventuresome. In 1809 they were forced to cede half their land to the United States, and indications were that this process would continue. Game soon became scarce as white settlements closed in around the perimeter of the Cherokee land. A group of tribe members, succumbing to the persuasions of the federal government to migrate to Arkansas, on the basis that white settlers would be "permanently forbidden" there, acceded at last on the promise this would be the "last" move they ever would be asked to make.

Those who moved to Arkansas, and thereby became known as the Western Cherokee, found open wilderness abundant with game and soon reinitiated their earlier mode of life. Sam Houston, the foster son of a Cherokee chief, had convinced his father to move the large Cherokee band of over 300 tribesmen from Tennessee to the Arkansas site. The new arrivals began immediately to develop their new Arkansas community, building homes, barns and granaries. But the federal government failed to honor its promise; after 1814 whites surged into the Arkansas area. These invaders consisted largely of squatters, outlaws and riffraff. When Arkansas was at last established as a Territory in 1819 its new legislature was no more willing than its predecessors in other states to recognize the Indians' land title. Briefly the federal government tried to fulfill its promise by evicting the encroaching whites from Indian lands, but the squatters quickly returned. They had little respect for property rights and the federal government was unwilling to commit military enforcement to fulfill its promises. As a result the Western Cherokee were victim to increasing violence and harassment. When at last they appealed to federal officials at Washington they were promised another "permanent" home on the plains, this beyond the western boundary of Arkansas:

> . . . which shall, under the most solemn guarantee of the United States, be and remain theirs forever—a home that shall never, in all future time, be embarrassed by having extended around it the lines, or placed over it the jurisdiction of a new territory, or a state. . . .

The Eastern Cherokee, having watched from their Georgia tribal grounds the disgraceful Arkansas episode, determined to stay where they were. This band was well on its way to "civilization," having developed schools and advanced farming and blacksmithing methods. One of their foremost achievements was that of Sequoyah, a brilliant Cherokee, who, without the advantage of formal schooling, composed a syllabic alphabet for the Cherokee language, an arduous task which took ten years. With the introduction of his eighty-six character alphabet a cultural revolution ensued in the Cherokee nation. Many tribesmen learned to read the language within months, and soon the first American Indian newspaper, the *Cherokee Phoenix* was being printed. Numerous books, including the Bible, were translated into Cherokee, and with its emphasis on education the nation made astounding advances, including the writing of a formal constitution and the establishment of an elected chief, senate, and house of representatives.

The Cherokee lands in Northwestern Georgia had been "guaranteed" the tribe by several treaties made with the United States. But when gold was discovered on Cherokee land Georgia yielded to the pressure of whites who wanted it. President Adams dispatched troops to defend the Indian land, but these troops were later withdrawn by his successor, the Indian-hating Andrew Jackson. In 1828 the State of Georgia declared all Cherokee rights to land void. The startled Cherokee fought this abrupt move by Georgia to nullify their rights through courts at every level and, ultimately, to the Supreme Court. The eloquent defense set forth by the Cherokee echoed, as well, for every other Indian tribe:

> The title of the Cherokee people to their lands is the most ancient, pure, and absolute known to man; its date is beyond the reach of human record; its validity confirmed by possession and enjoyment antecedent to all pretense of claim by any portion of the human race. . . . These attributes have never been relinquished by the Cherokee people and cannot be dissolved by the expulsion of the Nation from its own territory by the power of the United States government.

This plea, as noble as the Declaration of Independence, could not save the Cherokee. Though the Supreme Court ruled that the government's removal of the Cherokee from their tribal land was unconstitutional, President Jackson, contrary to his oath of office, refused to uphold the high court's decision. Jackson's inaction left Georgia free to banish the Cherokee Nation.

In 1830 Congress enacted the Indian Removal Act, which required Indians of all tribes residing east of the Mississippi River to relocate to government lands to the west of it. All earlier pretensions of permitting the Indians to peaceably occupy their lands had long since been exposed, and the federal government thereafter gave up even the attempt to appear benevolent. The Indian Removal Act did not prescribe force to achieve its ends, but force, in fact, was used. Indians who refused the order to move were warned their civil and property rights could no longer be guaranteed; in effect, they would be at the mercy of rapacious whites, who could seize their land and murder them without threat of government punishment. President Jackson thus intensified the pressure on Indians unwilling to relocate.

Through bribery, threats, and acts of murder, the federal militia under Jackson's supervision successfully effected 91 separate treaties consumating the relocation of Indians to Western lands. Not only the Cherokee, but dozens of other tribes were uprooted from their lands and transported to distant wilderness reaches of the West. They were moved like animals by their army escorts: many never completed the journey, starving or dying of disease along the way. The Cherokees made this bitter exodus over the "Trail of Tears" to their new home in Oklahoma, traveling the rugged country in winter blizzards. Without warm clothing, blankets and food, many Cherokee perished. A total of 100,000 Indians from the various tribes were moved west, where they again were "guaranteed" perpetual title to their new land by the government. Officials in Washington believed the rugged Western wilderness to be so uninhabitable that whites would never desire it. Yet the same fate was to befall the Indians west of the Mississippi as had the Cherokee in Georgia.

Americans soon discovered the land west of the Mississippi was not as remote as had earlier been supposed, particularly with the lure of the discovery of gold in California in 1848. This event triggered a new series of treaties designed to nullify Indian title to all lands lying in the path of travel routes to California. Wagon-trains bound for California and the promise of gold crossed Indian lands and expected the United States Army to defend them. The Indians again were confronted with the whites trespassing upon their lands. White hunters invaded Indian lands and slaughtered their buffalo, the plains Indians' major source of food. The death of millions of buffalo spelled the demise of their way of life more surely than the government ever could. Plains Indians wandered over vast areas in search of the migratory buffalo, and federal government soon started forcing more treaties upon them to confine their travels within the limits of a small reservation.

Earlier events of Indian history soon were repeated in the West. In Minnesota 40,000 white settlers invaded Sioux lands before the Indians finally retaliated by declaring war to protect their land. In the next weeks that followed 800 whites lost their lives, the price of encroaching upon Sioux land. The failure of the federal government to honor an annual annuity to the Indians also triggered the Sioux retaliation. The annuity was paid the Indians with the provision they remain on the reservation, the payment enabling them to buy food, since their small land area was inadequate to produce sufficient crops and was virtually devoid of wild game.

The great exodus of whites westward beyond the Mississippi soon set off the bloodiest Indian wars in American history. Fighting raged across the frontier for thirty years, from 1850 to 1880. It had been around 1840 that the plains Indians' culture had reached its peak, aided largely by the advantage of hunting from horseback. The greater number of buffalo which could be killed on horseback rather than on foot enabled the tribes to grow in population far beyond their previously limited numbers. Yet fifty years later these tribes had reached near extinction.

As treaties were made and broken by the federal government the Indians soon came to distrust everything promised by the white man. Perhaps the most infamous crime perpetrated against the Indians during these years of mounting distrust was the massacre at Sand Creek in 1864. It began when a band of 700 Cheyenne, in the hope of staving off further attack and war, gave up their weapons, assured of the government's amnesty and protection. They kept enough guns only for hunting. Camped near Sand Creek, the Cheyenne continued in this false sense of security. Within the fort nearby, the U.S. officers were amused, even relieved at the Indians' surrender of their guns for now they could attack and destroy the Cheyenne with little resistance. Colonel Chivington, in civilian life a Methodist minister, led the expedition. He set out against the Cheyenne with a force of 1,000 soldiers, leading into battle with the cry, "Scalps are what we're after . . . Kill and scalp all Indians— big ones and little ones."

Seeing the U.S. soldiers approach, the Cheyenne poured from their tents to greet them, secure in the protection they had been promised earlier by the governor, who was aware of the treacherous raid. Over their camp flew the American flag alongside the white flag of truce. As the militia approached the Cheyenne saw they were bearing weapons, and suddenly the surprise attack began. When the Indians realized what was happening they attempted to fight back, but it was hopeless. Over 300 Indians, including women and children, were brutally murdered. Others were scalped, some while they were still alive. One soldier seized a woman by the hair, cut out her heart, and carried it around on a stick, beaming. Others slashed out the Indian women's private parts and displayed them boldly on their hats and saddles. One hundred scalps taken that day were later displayed between acts to the applause of white theatre goers at the Denver Opera House.

The army's siege of the Cheyenne camp was horrendous and barbaric, yet other Indian bands had been massacred in the same grim manner. After this treachery at Sand Creek the plains were torn with war. The enraged Indians, seeking revenge, could no longer be pacified.

Meanwhile, white settlers, protected by the army, continued to trespass on and usurp Indian lands, game, and forestation, manifesting little respect for government treaties. In 1867 the federal government moved to establish two small reservations on which all plains Indians would be confined, one in the Black Hills of North Dakota, and the other in Oklahoma. While many Indians proceeded to the new reservations without resistance, others fought fiercely against the move for years. It no longer was merely a fight for their land, but one for their way of life, which they knew could not survive on the small reservations. Satanta, a Kiowa chief, stated it well:

> I don't want to settle. I love to roam the prairie. . . . These soldiers cut down my timber, they kill my buffalo, and when I see that, it feels as if my heart would burst with sorrow.

Resisting the new order to relocate, defiant Indians waged a guerrilla war in which 50 Indians successfully checkmated 3,000 federal troops. This bold protest against reservation life intensified as the corruption-riddled Bureau of Indian Affairs made life miserable for the new Indian residents on the reserves. Indian agents misappropriated funds allocated for Indian provisions and instead gave the Indians scant, rotten food. The "small reservation" policy also was destined to collapse as the discovery of gold in Dakota's Black Hills in 1874 drew scores of white prospectors onto the reservation. At first the

U.S. Army on orders from Washington attempted to keep out the gold-crazed hordes, but soon gave up. The Sioux again went on the warpath. General Custer's defeat at the Little Big Horn in 1876 was one of the last major battles the Sioux won. Indian resistance was slowly diminishing. This was due chiefly not to U.S. military aggression but to the wholesale destruction of buffalo, the Indians' vital sustenance. By 1881 the animals were almost extinct, leaving the Plains Indians starving and defeated. Nonetheless several Western tribes held out for years. The Nez Perce Indians of Oregon and Idaho outwitted the strategies of federal troops over more than a thousand miles of rugged country. They were finally subdued and relocated to a malarial region in far-off Oklahoma. Moving the Nez Perce, whose culture had evolved in the mountains and forests of the Northwest, to the barren steppes of Oklahoma was a cruel and mindless act.

The Apaches of the Southwest carried on their fight against government intervention until 1886 under the leadership of Geronimo, a skillful warrior driven by the almost fanatic rage born of years of white betrayal. When apprehended by government troops, Geronimo was arrested as a criminal, rather than recognized as the leader of a minority people desperately attempting to defend the land rightfully theirs.

In 1871 Congress declared that henceforth no Indian tribe or nation would be recognized as an independent power with whom the United States could legally contract treaties. This was perhaps an official admission that all such treaties had been worthless anyway, a waste of time and effort for both sides. The law stated that no tribe would be regarded as a sovereign nation. Thereafter, despite the new law, federal treaties with the Indians still were written but were cited by new terms such as "conventions." Thus, the Congressional control of Indian affairs was extended. The once-proud Indian nations were nations no longer; they now were considered wards of the United States government.

From the inception of the first white settlement on America's shores the Indians had been pushed ever further inland from the Atlantic Coast, and then, onto reservations in the East.

Next they all were moved west of the Mississippi. As the wave of white migration moved toward California, the Indians were removed to reservations in the West as well. Soon, the migrant whites invaded these Indian sanctums too. At last the American Indians' status as independent peoples was taken from them and they were reduced to being subjects of the U.S. government. In this capacity they were confined to small, often substandard reservations, where most remain today.

The federal government has also adopted other policies bearing on the fate of its native Indian peoples; without consulting the Indians, officials decided that reservation Indians should become independent farmers. Under the Dawes Severalty Act the reservations were subdivided into individual small parcels of land to be distributed among the tribe-members. When every living member of the tribe had received land, it was stipulated the surplus be offered for sale to non-Indian homesteaders, with the tribe retaining the proceeds from the sale. The Dawes Act was based upon a misconception—whereas the whites believed communal ownership of property was unnatural and that individual ownership among the Indians would foster attitudes of self-interest, the Indians had known only tribal ownership of lands for centuries. The program failed abominably. Under the Dawes Act system the Indians were soon reduced to poverty and failing health. It became apparent at last that the federal program so much in conflict with the traditional Indian commune environment had destroyed the last vestige of Indian life.

Over the years, the United States government negotiated some 360 treaties with approximately 200 Indian tribes and nations. Federal and state courts continually have affirmed these contracts as bound by the same solemn obligation as America's treaties with other world powers. Yet history confirms that the U.S. government violated nearly all of its treaties with the native Indians. In one such instance, only 20 years after a federal pact declared the Wichita Indians an independent nation, the government dispossessed the tribe of its entire land holdings. Many other similar treaties which acquired Indian lands for the United States were effected by the use of federal threats and military force. Often Indian chiefs were bribed. Even today the lands guaranteed many tribes in earlier treaties are being wrested or demanded from them. Treaties dating from 1791, for example, guarantee the Seneca Indians their Corn Planter reservation land perpetually or until they choose to sell it. When the U.S. Court of Appeals ruled the Seneca had to sell the land to enable a new public dam site, the Seneca balked. But the court held that progress in the public interest, supported by the law of eminent domain, made the ordered sale of Seneca land both lawful and necessary. Power projects, military installations and various other facilities have consistently taken precedence over Indian land rights and the integrity of governmental promises.

Despite the diminishing numbers of native Indians, their centuries-old values have endured. Their reverence for the stars and constellations, earth, trees, and skies; their reverence for animal and human life looms newly meaningful in this emerging age of ecology.

Not all the whites who participated in the events of history shaping the fate of the Indians were of the same self-seeking intent as Jackson, Harrison and Chivington. Others like Sam Houston and Davy Crockett worked diligently much of their lives in the defense and preservation of Indian rights. Crockett was elected to Congress from the state of Tennessee in 1828. He vigorously denounced Jackson's Indian Removal Policy, although he knew this unpopular stance would alienate voters. His forthright criticism cost him re-election to office. But several years later he ran again and was elected. His outspoken denunciation thereafter of the proposed Cherokee removal cost him another re-election. During the Congressional debate Crockett said:

> ... But should I be the only member of the House who voted against this bill, and the only man in the United States who disapproved of it, I would still vote against it, and it would be a matter of rejoicing till the day I die that I did it. A treaty is the highest law of the land, but there are those who do not find it so. They want to juggle with

the rights of the Indians and fritter them away. It's all wrong. It's not justice.

After again losing his Congressional seat for his defense of the Indians, Crockett moved to Texas and subsequently was killed at the Battle of the Alamo.

Sam Houston also was a friend to the Indians, almost from childhood. At the age of fifteen he went to live with the Cherokee in Tennessee and thereafter was adopted by Chief Jolly. Three years later Houston chastised an Indian agent for making sexual advances toward the Chief's young daughter. The incident aroused such hostility against Houston among the Indian agents that he was forced to return home. Later he served as Indian agent to Chief Jolly's Cherokee tribe during their relocation to Arkansas. While in this capacity Houston was sharply reprimanded by John Calhoun, Secretary of War, for appearing before him in Indian buckskin garb. Sam Houston ultimately became a lawyer and thereafter was elected to Congress. In 1827 he became Governor of Tennessee. From this position he made direct appeals to President Jackson in behalf of the Cherokee.

After fulfilling his gubernatorial term Houston went to Arkansas and became an "Indian" again. Corruption was rampant at the time among many of the Indian agents assigned to the Western Cherokee. Chief Jolly dispatched Houston to Washington as an Indian representative. There he addressed the tribe's grievances to President Jackson. Jackson agreed at last to dismiss several corrupt Indian agents. But his position on the plight of the Cherokee in Georgia remained inflexible.

Shortly thereafter the corrupt Indian agents were reinstated. The enraged Houston fired off letters of protest to Washington, but they went unanswered. Finally, in an effort to salve Houston, Jackson wrote him requesting that he go to Texas to confer with the hostile Comanche. Houston agreed and thereby was diverted from his persistent campaign in behalf of the Cherokee cause. Houston was later elected President of the Republic of Texas, and then governor of the state.

However, those whites who defended Indian rights in the

course of the young nation's emergence were both rare and largely ineffectual. In 1887 the Delaware chief Pachgantschilias, gave the Indians' view:

> I admit there are good white men, but they bear no proportion to the bad; the bad must be the strongest, for they rule. They do what they please. They enslave those who are not of their color, although created by the same Great Spirit who created them. They would make slaves of us if they could; but as they cannot do it, they kill us. There is no faith to be placed in their words. . . .

The U.S. State Department has recorded over fifty official wars waged by the government against the Indians. These wars, as well as the dispossession of the entire native Indian race, remain an open indictment of the American government and its people.

CHAPTER VII

America the Violent

When we envision the "America the Beautiful" of poets and lyricists we think of green, rolling hills, majestic mountains, sparkling blue lakes and streams, and verdant pine forests. But there is another America—America the Violent—a nation whose masses, over the course of some 300 years, have massacred her Indians, enslaved her blacks, waged a Civil War that killed 600,000 brothers, fomented massive, bloody riots, hurled atomic death upon Hiroshima and Nagasaki, and more recently, murdered the innocent Vietnamese villagers of My Lai. American aggression has assumed such diverse forms as political assassination, racial and religious riots, organized and individual crime. These major events of violence, rampant from the earliest days of the young republic, may startle those who see America as a land of equality, justice and tranquility.

Most recently, in the past decade, Americans have been alarmed by the impact of a rash of assassinations, an upsurge in rampant, violent crime, destructive riots in the ghettos and on college and university campuses. Even the nation's police and military were not exempt from implication in the brutality of the 1960's—they, too, were charged with riot-baiting and the injury and killing of innocent persons.

In but a single decade, four Presidential commissions were appointed to study the nation's growing manifestations of violence. The fact most were reticent to acknowledge was that violence has been almost traditional throughout the course of American history. It has loomed continuously, sometimes in greater, more fiery magnitude than at present.

This national characteristic was frankly defined by Professor Maxuell Brown in his report to the National Commission on the Causes and Prevention of Violence:

> We must recognize that, despite our pious official disclaimers, we have always operated with a heavy dependence upon violence in even our highest and most idealistic endeavors. We must take stock of what we have done rather than what we have said. When that is done, the realization that we have been an incorrigibly violent people is overwhelming.
>
> We must realize that violence has not been the action only of the ruffians and racists among us but has been the tactic of the most upright and respected of our people. Having gained this self-knowledge, the next problem becomes the ridding of violence, once and for all, from the ... American value system. ...

The seeming savagery of our times can be better understood in perspective if one is aware of the history of violence that has been an integral aspect of the American character since the inception of the nation. The birth of the nation by means of a Revolutionary war, the freeing of the slaves in the wake of a bloody civil conflict, the conquest and settlement of the frontiers by attack and seizure, the bitterly-won rights of farmers and laborers, and the increasing struggle to preserve law and order all have their roots in human violence.

America's military encounters are not considered here but rather the violence committed within the nation's cities and communities by and against her people. It is appropriate, then, that this topic be examined in the late nineteenth-century, a period marking one of the bloodiest non-military eras in American history, in which mobs of every allegiance swarmed the streets of the cities in frenzied fervor. Labor and racial violence were at a peak, and the Western frontier appeared to the world to be bathed in blood.

Her daily thousands of incidences of rape, murder, and mugging notwithstanding, America's citizen violence seems to reach its apogee in political assassination. Though the assassination of President John F. Kennedy shook the world, this most widely publicized form of violence is in America, almost commonplace. Presidents Lincoln, Garfield, and McKinley were also murdered while in office. Still other, less successful, attempts were made on the lives of Jackson, both Roosevelts, and Truman. And the United States Secret Service daily and routinely investigates innumerable threats against the President rarely revealed to the public. Many other prominent Americans also have been the victims of political assassins. These have included Huey Long, Robert Kennedy, Martin Luther King, Medgar Evers, and George Lincoln Rockwell, to name but a few. Unlike the President who may safely meet the public only under heavy Secret Service guard, these notables have not had attendant protection against the ever-present assassin.

The first attempt on a President's life occurred in 1835. A deranged citizen, Richard Lawrence, attempted to shoot Andrew Jackson, who himself had a reputation for violence garnered in war, brawls and shootings. Lawrence stepped in front of the President, aimed at his heart, and pulled the trigger. His pistol misfired. He immediately drew a second pistol which also misfired. President Jackson, saved by incredible luck, charged the assailant and attempted to beat him with a cane. Bystanders finally succeeded in protecting Lawrence from the wrathful President, and the would-be assassin was doomed to spend the rest of his life in a mental institution, imagining himself Richard III in the Tower of London. The President, in his efforts to beat Lawrence, reflects something of America's legitimization of violence. A national folk-hero, Jackson was a model to be emulated by the nation's young, and his deeds imparted an aura of respectability to violence.

Theodore Roosevelt also was an assassin's target. Retired after two terms as President, he ran again four years later for the coveted office on the Bull Moose ticket. During the election, while addressing a throng of enthusiastic supporters, Roosevelt was accosted and shot by John Schrank. The bullet penetrated four inches into his chest. The gunman was institutionalized for the rest of his life. But tough old Teddy would not be stopped by a bullet. He proceeded to deliver a fifty-minute speech. "It takes more than that to kill a Bull Moose," he proclaimed. "I give you my word. I do not care a rap about being shot, not a rap!" Roosevelt recovered with no serious after-effects and for the rest of his life carried the bullet in his body.

Franklin Roosevelt similarly escaped death from a would-be assassin's bullet. The gunman, Giuseppe Zangara, succeeded in shooting five people standing near Roosevelt during an appearance by the young President-elect, but failed in his effort to shoot FDR. Zangara later admitted he really had wanted to shoot President Hoover, but that it was too cold to journey to Washington, D.C., so instead he had settled on Roosevelt, yet to be inaugurated, who was visiting Florida. Zangara was not committed for mental treatment, as were his two assassin predecessors. Instead, convicted of murdering one of the bystanders at the Roosevelt gathering, he died in the electric chair. Nearly two decades later, in 1950, a nationalist Puerto Rican organization assigned two volunteers to kill President Harry Truman. The pair, Oscar Collazo and Griselio Torresola, attempted to shoot their way into Truman's residence, their guns blazing like desperados in a Western shootout. The President was saved by virtue of his heavy guard, but the attempt nevertheless cost two lives. Torresola and a police officer were killed, and Collazo and several others wounded. Collazo was tried for murder and sentenced to death, but President Truman later commuted his sentence to life imprisonment.

Perhaps better-known are the stories of the four successful Presidential assassinations. Abraham Lincoln, shot in Ford Theater at the zenith of his career by actor John Wilkes Booth, was the first American President to be assassinated. Chester Arthur was elevated to the Presidency sixteen years later when the bullet of a disappointed office-seeker struck down James Garfield after only a month in office. Twenty years after the death of Garfield, President William McKinley was shot by a young anarchist, Leon Czolgasz, and died from the abdominal wound eight days later. Three Presidential assassinations in only 36 years! The last such tragedy occurred in 1963 in Dallas when Lee Harvey Oswald allegedly shot President John F. Kennedy. The motive for Oswald's action was never fully established. Every American President and lesser office-holders as well, face the dread specter of assassination in violence-riddled America.

Another dark aspect of American history was the practice of "law enforcement" by terror and force in the Old West. This form of enforcement, denying the accused due process of a fair trial, relied heavily on capital punishment through lynching. Lynching, in contrast to stoning or guillotining, is a peculiarly American innovation, first popularized by the vigilantes. Though many criminals were executed, so, too, were the innocent among them, denied even the justice of a fair trial. In one such episode the vigilantes hanged an entire six-man jury because they had acquitted a man the vigilantes believed to be guilty. Then they hanged the acquitted man from the same tree.

They should have sought to establish order through jurisprudence, legislation, and local law enforcement. Their brand of "justice," which was so swift and certain, sowed precedents which today are yielding a bitter harvest. Thus, countless Americans, emulating the vigilantes of an earlier day, believe themselves justified in taking the law into their own hands if their cause is just. As the Ku Klux Klan may loom as a grim reminder of vigilante "justice," so students and minority-group interests which seek to gain positive goals through the use of violence also are working in the vigilante tradition.

Along with the vigilante, the West added still another violent stereotype to the national heritage that was also to arouse adulation for generations—the murderer "hero." Some of these killer heroes were revered as "good," others, condemned as "evil." Both were to grip the national imagination. But the truth is, none of them were heroic; they were, on the whole, deplorable and cowardly killers. Jesse James, for example, is deified in public legends as a sort of American Robin Hood. Nothing could be farther from the truth. A sulking, mean, and sadistic killer, Jesse was known to the people of his time for what he was. Not even his outlaw peers respected him. At the zenith of his murderous career, James was gunned down by members of his own gang in their ardor to obtain the reward on his head. Another legendary figure, Billy the Kid, was branded "a dirty little killer" by his contemporaries. A seemingly homicidal maniac who reveled in killing, he chiefly doted on unarmed victims and shooting people in the back.

The reputation of Wild Bill Hickok, lauded by historians as a frontier marshal and outstanding marksman bent on law and order, also does not hold up under scrutiny. Hickok killed some five men in his life, three of these unarmed. In one such encounter, as a sheriff, he inadvertently shot and killed his deputy. A great braggart, Hickok thereby developed a reputation for himself. His career ended abruptly when he was shot in the back by a young man who also was seeking a reputation.

One famous frontiersman, Judge Roy Bean, was known as "The Law West of the Pecos." An El Paso newspaper article of 1884 indicated the kind of "justice" which was often meted out in the frontier West:

> Somebody killed a Chinaman and was brought up standing before the irrepressible Roy, who looked through two or three dilapidated law books from stem to stern and he'd finally turned the culprit loose remarking that he'd be d——d if he could find any law against killing a Chinaman.[1]

These "heroes" were not the West's only practitioners of violence; it seemed to be the tradition, even the religion, of the lusty, brawling frontier. Cattle ranchers fought other cattlemen over such issues as open range versus fenced-in pastures. Both killed sheepmen because their animals grazed too close to the roots. All three groups killed rustlers and squatters, and everyone killed Indians. The Wild West long has been glorified in books, movies, and TV epics, but, in truth, its decades of senseless violence had no romantic mystique or adventure for those who lived and died then—it was sordid killing.

1. From B. A. Botkin, *A Treasury of American Folklore.* New York: Crown Publishers, 1944.

Labor riots have been yet another source of violence and bloodshed in the nation's unquiet history. The United States has witnessed 160 labor riots of such fury and magnitude as to be uncontrollable by the police, requiring military intervention. These labor uprisings, concentrated chiefly in the late nineteenth-century, added yet another strata to the depths of the nation's violence.

In 1874, organized labor's Tompkins strike was answered by extreme police brutality, a commonplace reaction in earlier eras when government sought to squelch or subdue worker uprisings. The workers, who had repeatedly been denied permits to hold a mass meeting, at last succeeded in obtaining the required sanction. As the crowd gathered, however, the members were not aware the permit had just been revoked. Suddenly, mounted policemen rode into the center of the throngs, ordered them to disperse, and then galloped brutally through the crowd, clubbing the workers as they fled in every direction. The police took chase on their horses, clubbing everyone who ran before them. They seemed to be as crazed as the fleeing mob, striking out madly and indiscriminately. Labor leader Samuel Gompers termed their actions "an orgy of brutality."

Prior to 1877 labor strikes had been confined to the local level, but in that year the first nationwide strike erupted, called by the railroad workers. The grievance largely stemmed from poor working conditions and a wage-cut protest in the wake of a depression. The railroad walkout triggered a series of violent rail strikes which were to quickly convulse the entire country and lead many to believe that worker revolution was imminent. The wildfire strike put two-thirds of the nation's railroads at a standstill. Railroad workers in Baltimore refused to let the trains move. They were confronted by the local militia, and large-scale violence soon ensued. The workers set fire to the railway station and attacked the militia with stones and clubs. The militia returned their fire with a barrage of bullets. The militia was deadly serious, as attested by the deaths of eleven workers.

At about the same time, the bloodiest foray since the Civil

War occurred in Pittsburgh. Militia and railroad strikers met head-on in a freight yard, and twenty rail workers were killed. When word of the killings spread through Pittsburgh the 1,000-man militia was set upon by several thousand outraged local citizens. The surrounded soldiers fought their way through the crowds and fled the city, suffering about twenty-five casualties. The explosive mob then looted and destroyed some 2,000 railroad cars and numerous buildings.

The mob moved on, pillaging the city. The ultimate destruction was to total over five-million dollars. A call-up of federal troops poured into Pittsburgh and subdued the riot, but not before it had triggered outbreaks in other areas of the country. Once federal troops were committed by President Hayes to subdue the growing nationwide violence, the rail strike was a lost cause. Troops suppressed worker uprisings in one city after another, and soon the trains were moving again. The great railroad strike of 1877 was over, but the nation had witnessed its first national labor upheaval, and with it, twenty-six deaths in Pittsburgh alone and millions of dollars in property damage.

Nine years later, at Haymarket Square in Chicago, some 1,500 workers gathered to rally for an eight-hour working day. Police attempted to disperse the crowds. A bomb exploded and rioting ensued. Eleven were killed and over one hundred wounded. While the identity of the bomb-thrower was never established, eight agitators were arrested and seven of them subsequently were sentenced to death. Four of the convicted were hanged before a new governor, convinced that the trial had been unfair, pardoned the three who were still imprisoned.

In 1892, another major strike at the Carnegie Steel Company plant in Homestead, Pennsylvania gripped the nation. Thousands of strikers, protesting recent wage-cuts, ringed the Carnegie plant and refused to let non-striking workers enter the building. When local law-enforcement officers proved ineffectual in their efforts to disperse the strikers, 300 Pinkerton guards were brought in to gain access to the factory. Seven were killed by the swirling mob, and the rest surrendered and withdrew. At this point the federal government moved in 8,000 troops and soon subdued the riot. The violence of the strikers served to further alienate public sentiments from the unions. This dwindling of public support was to weaken the cause of organized labor nationwide.

The Pullman strike of 1894 in Chicago, another worker protest against wage-cuts, drew a response from management to squelch the walkout by employing force rather than peaceful arbitration. Again the action triggered large scale violence. American Socialist leader Eugene Debs, who had called for the strike and boycott against the Pullman Company, was subsequently jailed. President Cleveland, without a request from Governor J. P. Altgeld of Illinois, immediately dispatched troops to the scene on the pretext of moving the mail. Governor Altgeld protested the call out, but the troops moved in over his objection and widespread violence ensued. In Chicago alone, twenty-five persons were killed, sixty were seriously wounded, and millions of dollars in property was destroyed. The violence was quelled only by the total force of some 14,000 army troops!

Labor uprisings and resultant violence, which never could be blamed solely on the strikers, management, or the intervening police, continued in the United States for the next several decades. In one, a miners' walkout, the governor of Idaho who broke the strike was killed by an assassin hired by the mine workers' union. In 1913, a strike at a Ludlow, Colorado coal mine erupted into a battle said to be as bloody as any in wartime. The state militia, brought in to maintain order, joined in the frenzy themselves. The officers seemed to lose control as the soldiers turned into an unruly mob, pillaging the miners' homes and destroying everything they could not loot. At the grim conclusion, death-toll estimates in Ludlow ran as high as 175. Many of the victims were women and children.

Labor violence did not end with World War I, but continued on through the Great Depression. During this era of bleak, widespread unemployment, workers were joined by farmers in uprisings and violent public protests. Already cited have been similar farmers' rebellions prior to the Revolution, and two others—Shays' Rebellion and The Whiskey Insurrection —when the nation was young.

The Great Depression found farmers hard pressed to meet their financial obligations. Many, destitute and confronted with foreclosure, faced the loss of their only means of livelihood. When sheriffs attempted to foreclose such mortgages and dispossess farmers from their land, they were often met by mobs bearing clubs and pitchforks and forced to retreat. Judges issuing foreclosure notices were threatened with death or injury, and the seething masses of discontented farmers were near rebellion in many areas. The New Deal, under Franklin D. Roosevelt, listened to these desperate voices and probably averted a major collapse of America's agrarian society. Hungry farmers and workers, long accustomed to resorting to violence, doubtless would have erupted into a nationwide rebellion had not the Roosevelt administration reacted with speed and determination to ease their plight. A series of job and welfare programs were quickly launched to stimulate the labor economy, offset hunger and disease, and aid the nation's impoverished farmers. By gaining the trust of labor and farmers through these emergency measures, FDR averted further violence and reversed the rampaging course of a severe economic plunge.

Another form of violence common in American history, but less in evidence today, is the aggression generated by religious dogma, which had its national beginning with the Puritan persecution of dissenters. The major victims of religious violence in 19th-Century America were the Roman Catholics, who were chiefly persecuted from 1830 to 1860. In one such incident, a Catholic convent was burned by a wild mob in 1834. The mob allowed the nuns and novitiates to escape, then threw all the furniture from the convent windows. Barrels of oil brought by the mob ignited the building quickly. Fire-fighters sped to the scene but were not allowed to extinguish the holocaust, which quickly gutted the building. Thereafter all of the rioters who had been arrested for arson were acquitted, despite conclusive evidence against them, and walked out of the court room to the cheers of a crowd.

Extraordinary intolerance against Roman Catholics continued to be exhibited throughout the next decade, stirred by newspapers, magazines, the rantings of Protestant churchmen, and even an American political party, the Native Americans. In 1844, the City of Brotherly Love, Philadelphia, was transformed into a battleground pitting Protestants and Irish-Catholics. The hostility had begun when local Roman Catholics voiced opposition to the use of the Protestant Bible in public schools, petitioning instead for the use of a Catholic Bible by Catholic children. The protest quickly fanned hateful rumors, including the unreasonable fear that the Pope intended to conquer America. One evening, a mob of non-Catholics instigated a riot by attacking the homes of Irish-Catholics, and soon destruction and death spread throughout Philadelphia. When Catholic homes and buildings were set ablaze, the city firemen made no attempt to extinguish the flames. A Catholic Church was ignited, and as the steeple cross fell crashing to the ground, the onlooking crowds cheered wildly. That most of them were "Christians" and the cross was their symbol, too, seemed to make no difference to the mob. Martial law was declared at last and order restored, but not before a dozen were killed and some fifty seriously injured.

Anti-Catholicism continued in the 1850's as the Know-Nothing Party gained in influence, campaigning largely on a platform of bigotry against the Catholics. The party platform urged the removal of Catholics from every phase of American life and their ultimate deportation to Ireland. Know-Nothing mobs swarmed around polling places on election days to prevent Irish-Catholics and other foreign-born citizens from voting. As a result pitched battles often erupted around the public polls, and voting became a dangerous endeavor, especially for Catholics. During one such election-day riot in St. Louis, ten were killed and thirty seriously wounded. A year later, in Louisville, Kentucky, a mob led by Know-Nothings attempted to use a cannon to destroy a Catholic Church but was turned back by one of its leaders. The crowd proceeded to the Irish quarter, where they burned houses and killed at least twenty Catholics.

Catholic persecution continued until the end of the 19th Century. Another religious group came under heavy fire at the same time—the Mormons. In 1838 a settlement of members of the Church of Latter-Day Saints in Missouri was set upon by an angry mob who demanded they leave the area. The action had been triggered by an advertisement in a Mormon newspaper which invited "free" Negroes to join the sect and settle on Mormon land. Local residents were infuriated. The band of Mormons begged their attackers for ten days in which to consider the demand. Instead, they were given fifteen minutes and then set upon. At this point the Mormons promised they would vacate within a day, whereupon the aggressors went wild with rage. They beat the Mormons and pillaged and burned their homes. One group of eighteen Mormons, including women and children, was slaughtered by the mob. When a small Mormon boy pleaded for mercy, a callous citizen blew his brains out. Missouri Governor Boggs sided with the mob, declaring, "The Mormons must be treated as enemies, and must be exterminated or driven from the state if necessary, for the public peace."

The outcast Mormons migrated to Nauvoo, Illinois, where they rapidly built a thriving settlement. The surrounding community, motivated by growing religious hatred, attacked the colony and again forced the Mormons to flee their homes in the wake of murder and looting. Mormon leader, Joseph Smith, and his brother, Hyrum, were arrested and charged with treason. In 1844, at Carthage, they were set upon and lynched by an angry mob.

The Mormon band proceeded to Utah, where they found a permanent home. But America's anti-Mormon violence had not ended. Like the Catholics, the Mormons eventually reacted to their tormentors with violence of their own. In one such instance in 1857 a settlement of Mormons, which had previously allowed many wagon trains to pass through its territory, stopped the Fancher Party bearing a flag of truce. The Mormons explained they wanted to escort the train through hostile Indian country. Instead they placed the travelers under guard and disarmed them. On a prearranged signal, the Mormons massacred the entire party, including women and children. Violence had answered violence.

Racial violence also has been widespread in America, victimizing every minority group, including blacks, Mexican-Americans, and Asian-Americans. Such widespread persecution, though without government sanction, has extracted a bloody toll, spreading hatred and death over the nation almost from its infancy. An early reaction to black persecution, the slave rebellion, was a common occurrence during the early years of the Republic. Southerners, justifiably fearful of such rebellions, kept large arsenals on hand to subdue rioting slaves, who had virtually no other means of gaining freedom. While rebellious slaves were executed, runaways were treated almost as badly, though they posed no physical threat to the whites. Law officers tracked down runaways with bloodhounds. When found the escapees were beaten mercilessly and even branded.

The most famous slave rebellion was instigated by a black Southern slave, Nat Turner. In 1831, Turner, believing he had been chosen by God to win freedom for the oppressed blacks, began by murdering his master and the master's family. He was soon joined by other slaves, and they murdered slave-owners and their families as they traveled. Within a day Turner's group had murdered sixty whites, over half of them children. State and federal troops soon surrounded the rebels and over one hundred slaves were killed in the ensuing battle, while many more were captured and lynched. The rebellion, termed by historians Nat Turner's Revolt, claimed over two hundred lives.

Two earlier slave uprisings surpassed the Turner Revolt in the number of slaves rebelling, if not in bloodshed. In 1800, Gabriel Prosser led 1,100 slaves on a march to Richmond, set on destroying the city. A heavy storm temporarily dispersed the blacks, enabling white troops to surround and capture them in small groups. At least thirty-five of their leaders were executed. The other major slave rebellion was led by Denmark Vesey, a bright, liberated former slave. Vesey had bought his own freedom from slavery, and, employed as a carpenter, he devoted much of his leisure time to studying revolutions. For twenty years, he plotted a slave revolt, fervently determined that other slaves should gain the freedom he had. Vesey recruited followers among local black slaves and at last organized a large group ready to revolt. At the eleventh hour the plan was betrayed by a slave confiding in his master. The rebels were arrested, and forty-seven, including Vesey, were executed.

Another episode in America's long history of racial violence was the New York Draft Riot of 1863, the largest in a series of riots that shook the city after 1830. Though non-racial motives also triggered the uprising, it was the biggest and bloodiest race riot in the nation's history. The riots began as a middle-class protest against conscription into the Union Army. The draft laws enabled young men to avoid conscription by paying a tribute of $300, and few except the wealthy could afford to do so. This discrimination enraged the city's working class. A mob gathered at the draft center and destroyed its files and equipment, then marched on a gun factory and captured it after a long and bloody fight. Well armed with pilfered guns, the mob quickly spread into the city, attacking and looting the homes of the wealthy who had the means to exempt themselves from the draft. Then the riot turned on the city's blacks, since the rioters identified the local Negroes with Southern slaves for whose emancipation the Northern whites were being drafted and sent to war. Nor was the draft the only source of frustration associated with the blacks. The whites were also fearful of losing their jobs if the war succeeded in emancipating Southern slaves whom they believed would come north by the thousands, willing to work for low wages. Thus local blacks were attacked wherever they were found, and often beaten to death. One such victim, after being beaten and lynched, was burned by the mad rioters, who danced around the flaming corpse, yelling and cursing. Army troops, some ordered directly from the Battle of Gettysburg, were able to quell the rioters only after four days of bloody fighting. The soldiers used cannons and Gatling guns in the narrow New York streets and finally with brutal battle tactics subdued the rioters. The New York draft riots were the bloodiest riots in the nation's history.

An extraordinary amount of racial violence against blacks also was rampant after the Civil War. The growing Ku Klux Klan murdered countless numbers in an effort to discourage the newly freed blacks from voting, creating in the South an atmosphere of terror.

The frequent black lynchings throughout the South, entailing a relatively merciful method of murder compared to some employed by the frenzied mobs, were often followed by widespread riots against entire black communities. Many blacks were tortured unmercifully, being dismembered bit by bit, and then, while still barely alive, were set on fire. The burning body and charred corpse often served as a spectacle of entertainment for thousands, including young children brought to the scene to "enjoy" the sight. Southern lynchings and riots often stemmed from allegations of a black's violation of a white woman, whereas Northern riots and lynchings, which also were shockingly frequent, did not resort to such an excuse.

In 1919 America was again convulsed by racial uprisings against the blacks. But this time blacks fought back in groups, and what had previously been one-way aggressions were suddenly transformed into battles. Such violent racial confrontations have continued to our day, with blacks changing from the role of passive victim to that of combatant and, more recently, aggressor in violence. The Los Angeles' Watts riot of 1965 culminated with a toll of thirty-four dead, 1,000 injured and 4,000 jailed. Property damage approached forty-million dollars. Just as decades of religious violence seemed to have come full-circle to lash back at the nation, so had the generations of violence perpetuated against America's blacks.

But the blacks were not the sole targets of racial uprisings. Other ethnic minority groups have also endured the murderous wrath of America's majority. The Chinese, vital in the development of the West Coast, were frequent victims of racial uprisings. Chinese immigrants in Rock Springs, Wyoming were treated inhumanely by the local citizenry for years. Eventually a full-scale attack erupted against the Chinese community.

When federal troops were at last dispatched to restore order in the wake of death and destruction, the local newspaper lashed out vehemently in its editorials against the government protection of the Chinese-Americans.

Widespread national violence against the Chinese subsided only when Congress enacted the "Chinese exclusion" law of 1882 and subsequent restrictive measures in 1917, 1921, and 1924 limiting the immigration of the Chinese to America. Japanese immigration into America was also restricted by similar federal legislation.

No discussion of violence in America would be complete without mention of three ugly blemishes today: student violence, ghetto riots, and crime in the cities. Much has been said about the link between violence and today's spoiled youth and radical left-wingers. Unfortunately, these and others have learned too well the silent message that courses through era after era of American history: "Violence can serve a good cause well." Thus, intent on changing America, many today accept uncritically the most destructive tenet within their American heritage—the myth that violence provides a short and easy route to desirable goals. Blacks in the ghetto at times also echo this myth, viewing violence as their only real course to equality and recognition, and to all that comprises the white man's "better way-of-life." In contrast, in recent decades the militant members of the far-right have largely refrained from displays of violence. Unlike their leftist counterpart groups, such as the Weathermen, America's organized right-wing thus far has only spoken out. It has not resorted to large-scale use of the bombs and weapons many leftists have stockpiled, instead succumbing only to violent rhetoric. For example, William Patrick, addressing the United Republicans of California, said, "I disagree with those who want to impeach Earl Warren. I think we should hang him." And an American Legion audience was told by retired Air Force General Robert Scott that a military takeover of the United States might become necessary if the nation's politicians failed to control lawlessness. However reprehensible, such talk does not compare in destructiveness with the riots and bombings staged by the far-left.

Violent crime in America, particularly in the cities, is also a national problem of monumental proportions and one that is on the rise. Most crimes of violence, national statistics show, are not committed by maniacs, misfits, or hardened criminals, but by average citizens—a man against his family, friends, neighbors, or business associates. Perhaps the most shocking form of individual violence is the mass murder. Such baseless slaughters, like those committed by Charles Whitman in Texas (thirteen victims), Richard Speck in Chicago (eight murdered), Juan Corona in California (25 dead), and the Houston, Texas sex-sadism slayings (28 murdered) are not new phenomena. Between 1890 and 1894, rooming-house owner H. A. Holmes murdered about twenty-seven of his boarders; then, through an agent, sold the bodies to medical schools for dissection. These mass murders characteristically are senseless crimes with no rational motive.

Organized crime also is a national dilemma, staggering in scope, which costs the United States some fifty billion dollars a year. But the cost to the nation is more than a financial one. Today the Mafia looms as the biggest business in the world. This gargantua has vast political control, as well as a god-like hold over life and death in America. In an earlier era underworld gangs killed each other off in wholesale numbers; but today they have extended their terror tactics to the public. The Mafia harasses, disables, and even murders those who bear witness against its heinous crimes, as well as legitimate business competitors, and others who get in its way.

In one such instance, during the 1960's, the Mafia clashed head-on with the huge national A & P supermarket grocery chain over the issue of A & P stores stocking a Mafia-made detergent. When A & P officials refused to stock the product despite Mafia pressure and threats, several multimillion dollar A & P warehouses were razed. One store manager was murdered in cold blood. The case was but a single instance of the Mafia's persuasive business tactics nationwide. America's law-enforcement agencies including the F.B.I., have been virtually ineffectual in halting the underworld's organized, well-planned corruption, today rampant in every major city in the United States.

And today, violence continues to prevail at every level of American life. While the Declaration of Independence cites man's "inalienable right" to "life, liberty and the pursuit of happiness," in the two centuries since that right was officially declared America has not ensured these privileges to everyone. For the countless victims of violence in America, these words of the great Declaration are merely that—words. During the twentieth-century alone some 800,000 persons in America have been killed by privately-owned guns. This toll exceeds the total number of Americans killed in all of the foreign wars in which our nation has participated. And as violence continues to mount on the nation's contemporary scene the number is destined to soar.

CHAPTER VIII

American Imperialism and the War on Spain

The period in America history beginning in 1890 is often termed "the Age of Imperialism." During this era of acquisition, America, like the Great European powers, rapidly extended her political control over lesser territories. Though some of these were holdings purchased from other powerful nations, America's rule can nevertheless be termed "imperialism" since these territories were chiefly acquired and ruled without the consent of their peoples. The beginnings of American imperialism extend further back in her history. The Mexican War was an act of overt imperialism initiated by the U.S. to gain the territories of California and New Mexico.

The incipient concept of imperialism was first expressed by President Monroe in 1825 in the famed Monroe Doctrine. Though this doctrine was no more than a public speech when first pronounced, it continues to influence American foreign policy even today. The Monroe Doctrine has often been used by American leaders to justify their aggressive interference in the affairs of other Western Hemisphere nations. In recent years it was used in an effort to explain America's illegal acts against Cuba.

In essence the Monroe Doctrine proclaimed that the United States would not interfere in the Affairs of Europe, and that in turn, the U.S. expected European powers to limit their activities within the Western Hemisphere. Monroe stated that these foreign powers could retain the Western colonies they possessed, but were forbidden to acquire new colonies in the Western Hemisphere. For many years this outspoken directive was largely ignored in both hemispheres. It was obvious that the United States, whose own Capitol had been overrun by foreign invaders only a decade earlier, did not have the power to police the entire Western Hemisphere. In fact European statesmen said the Monroe Doctrine was "worthy of only the most profound contempt." Latin American leaders also elected to ignore it, knowing they could not rely on the pledge of United States military support in the event of foreign attack. The European's disdain for the doctrine is evinced by several notable examples of anti-Doctrinal "transgressions." England's occupation of the Falkland Islands; her aggressive actions in Central America; and the French blockade of Argentina and Mexico. None of these acts, though clearly counter to the Monroe Doctrine, drew a murmur of protest from Washington.

Latin America knew her greatest hope of protection against encroaching foreign powers lay not with the United States but with England and her powerful Navy. Because America's Monroe Doctrine was mere political rhetoric, it did not cement closer ties between the U.S. and other Western Hemisphere nations. Indeed, when these nations sought to secure treaties with the United States that would clearly define and guarantee the specifics of the Doctrine as they applied to them, the United States flatly refused.

Further undermining the Monroe Doctrine was the fact that it was based on the faulty premise that all areas of North and South America were settled, since it "forbid" all new colonization on either continent, as well as action by any foreign power to reconquer a former colony that had gained independence. Monroe's declaration might have represented a commendable beginning toward inscribing the right of self-determination had the two continents indeed been wholly settled and the sovereignity of each of the areas established. However, the opposite was true: many areas of North and South America were still unsettled, and others were in dispute. Thus the doctrine proved to be colored with American self-interest. Many U.S. leaders, such as John Quincy Adams, believed the United

States one day would extend to all of North America and to Cuba. It is evident that the Monroe Doctrine was largely motivated by such imperialistic ambitions.

Though America could not hope to back up the self-seeking promulgation with real force, several factors wholly unrelated to the Doctrine served to minimize foreign encroachments on the Western Hemisphere for years to come: Britain, which boasted the world's greatest military might, particularly in her dominance of the seas, had no desire to see competitor nations increase their American holdings; at the same time the major European powers were concentrating their energies in Asian and African colonization, and much of Latin America was achieving independent stability.

With time the Doctrine grew in its generality and blatant self-interest. One addendum made around 1870 and called the "no-transfer principle," forbade the transfer of new-world colonies by one nation to another. This corollary went so far as to declare that a foreign power could not sell her new-world territories even if she so desired, though the United States in similar dealings purchased territories such as Alaska from foreign nations.

A further extension of the Doctrine occurred in 1895 when the United States intervened between Britain and Venezuela in their boundary dispute in South America. Though Britain ended up with the majority of the disputed territory, the United States had seemingly declared to the world that she was the self-appointed arbiter of all European conflicts in the Western Hemisphere. This presumptuous stand served only to spur resentment against the U.S. in Latin America, and Europe voiced critical charges against the American intervention.

Further enlargement of the Doctrine occurred with Theodore Roosevelt's corollary, which appointed the United States military to act as an international police force throughout the Western Hemisphere. Under this corollary U.S. Marines were landed in Nicaragua, and the United States seized control of customs in that country, as well as in the Dominican Republic and Honduras. The practice continued under Wilson, who forcibly intervened in Haiti and the Dominican Republic, declaring America's desire to help "the people of those republics in establishing honest and responsible governments to such extent as may be necessary in each particular case."

Individual Latin American countries as well as Pan-American Conferences went strongly on record to oppose American meddling in their internal affairs. America was ultimately forced by growing world resentment to outwardly agree to abide by the principles of self-determination, but the events of recent history show that she has repeatedly intervened in the politics of neighboring nations. Her actions in Guatemala and in the Cuban Bay of Pigs invasion are but two examples of her unending efforts to exert her will in the affairs of other countries.

The Monroe Doctrine set the stage for later acts of American imperialism. From 1860 to 1918, the United States annexed numerous territories without conducting general plebiscites to determine if the inhabitants wanted their lands to become part of the United States. And most of these territorial residents were taxed by the U.S. without their prior consent. Nor were these territories, once annexed, accorded political representation in America's democratic system.

In 1867, U.S. Secretary of State Seward purchased the territory of Alaska for a mere pittance. The people of Alaska were neither consulted nor did they vote on this annexation. This territory was the first United States acquisition which did not physically adjoin its existing states or territories.

Thereafter all inhabitants of Alaska except the native Eskimos were declared citizens of the United States and said to be granted all rights and privileges that status implies. Since 27,000 of the then 29,000 inhabitants of Alaska were Eskimos, however, the great majority were not accorded the rights guaranteed in the U.S. Constitution. Nor does history indicate that the 2,000 so-called "citizens" enjoyed any of the benefits of U.S. citizenship, either. Alaska was placed under U.S. military rule for a decade. No provision was made for its "citizens" to vote and no civil government was established. The U.S. Army introduced whiskey and syphilis into the territory as its only legacies to Alaska.

135

Thereafter, Alaska was not exploited by the United States; it was simply ignored. When, for example, Indians threatened to attack the small Alaskan coastal community of Sitka, the "citizens" appealed to Congress for aid. No help was forthcoming. Thus they appealed to Russia and Britain, both of whom responded immediately with military aid.

Such neglect was to characterize America's ownership of Alaska. For example, the first governor of Alaska, appointed in Washington, D.C. rather than elected by the Alaskan people, spent only a few days of his two-year term in Alaska. The citizens of Alaska were not permitted full representation in the U.S. government or, indeed, in their own for nearly 100 years from the time of Alaska's annexation by the U.S. Because of their inability to participate in their own government, the Alaskan peoples were little more than colonial subjects of the United States.

In 1867 the United States annexed another non-contiguous holding, the Midway Islands, two small atolls in the Pacific covering only a few square miles and situated approximately midway between Asia and North America. These islands had no native inhabitants and were thus legitimate acquisitions. The same year Secretary of State Seward negotiated the purchase of the Virgin Islands from Denmark, but the U.S. Senate refused to ratify the treaty and America did not acquire these Islands until 1917. Though the 35,000 inhabitants of the Virgin Islands directly elect a local Senate, they enjoy only limited democracy, even today. Their governor is appointed by the President of the United States and serves an indefinite term. They have no vote in U.S. Presidential elections nor representation in Congress. Though citizens of the United States, they have no voice in its government.

After Secretary of State Seward retired from office, America's territorial expansion ceased until 1889, the year the U.S. signed an agreement with Germany and Great Britain making Samoa a joint protectorate of all three nations. Thereafter America assumed exclusive rights to approximately one-half of the Samoan islands, and in 1929 officially annexed them. The islands are now collectively called American Samoa. Their

2,000 inhabitants have no representative in the U.S. Congress and do not vote in U.S. Presidential elections. Their governor is not elected but appointed by the U.S. Secretary of the Interior. The Samoans have not been granted United States citizenship.

America's expansionism and international involvement increased sharply beginning about 1890. Spurred by the incredible recent growth of its economy the U.S. adopted a bellicose attitude in its international relations. As a result it nearly plunged into war with Chile in 1891. Anti-Yankee feelings at the time were running high in that South American country, when, in Valparaiso, a small Chilean coastal town, a feud erupted between a band of American sailors and the local citizenry. A mob of Chileans attacked the sailors, two of whom were killed. When the Chilean government refused to make reparations for the deaths and injuries caused by the mob, U.S. President Harrison dispatched a war message to Congress. Realizing that the minor incident was not worth risking full-scale war, the Chilean government issued an official apology and made reparations. But America's belligerence, though gaining Chile's capitulation, was to have long-term detrimental effects. The widely publicized humiliation of Chile wrought massive Latin American resentment against the United States.

Two years later America again teetered on the verge of war in South America, this time in Venezuela. Between that country and British Guiana lay a region whose ownership had long been contended by the two nations. President Grover Cleveland decided to intervene in the border dispute in behalf of Venezuela, demanding that the British submit the dispute to arbitration under a U.S. threat of war. Despite this, Britain ignored the communique for months. Answering at last, it pointed out that the Monroe Doctrine had no status in international law and refused to submit the matter to arbitration. Provoked, U.S. officials set out to determine the correct border on their own, prepared to declare war if their decision were not accepted. Britain, however, had no desire to go to war over a small isolated area of South America and finally agreed to submit the dispute to a tribunal. Ironically, the judges awarded almost the entire region in dispute to Great Britain. This blustering approach to foreign diplomacy was soon to plunge America into the Spanish-American War.

In the interim the United States resumed its acquisition of overseas territories. Negotiations for annexation of the Hawaiian Islands were first initiated in 1854, but were terminated by the United States when the Hawaiians insisted on being directly admitted to the Union as a state. Though the islands were highly desirable possessions, Congress refused to sanction their requested admission to the Union with full statehood status.

A white islander minority had long held political control of the Islands. When Queen Liliuokalani assumed the throne in 1891, she initiated a "Hawaii for Hawaiians" movement which overthrew the domestic white rule. Aggrieved by their sudden loss of long-time political control and fearful of further deterioration of their economic power, the militant white minority planned a secret coup and requested American aid. The coup was executed successfully with the help of American troops furnished by the U.S. ambassador to Hawaii. Queen Liliuokalani was deposed and a white provisional government installed, which immediately appealed to the United States for annexation. But President Cleveland, on hearing of the coup, was shocked to learn that U.S. forces had figured in the overthrow of Hawaii's legitimate government, a breach of diplomacy and an act of unprovoked military assault. When the President also learned of the native Hawaiians' opposition to U.S. annexation, he refused to sanction the acquisition.

President Cleveland thereafter considered restoring Queen Liliuokalani to power, but decided this could be achieved only by force, so firmly had the white islanders reestablished their rule. Not wishing to again involve American forces in Hawaii, Cleveland decided against the intervention, though he considered America's role in the coup a disgrace. Hawaii continued for several years as an independent nation. On assuming office, President McKinley moved to annex the islands, despite the desire of native Hawaiians to remain independent. When the U.S. Senate refused to support McKinley's bid for annexation he presented the bill to a joint session of both houses. It was ratified in 1898.

Thus, the Hawaiian people were made U.S. citizens, but Hawaii remained a U.S. territory for fifty-nine years before being admitted to statehood. Over those years Hawaii's territorial legislature repeatedly petitioned the U.S. Congress for admission to statehood, but to no avail. Hawaiian residents were required to pay taxes but had no representation in Congress, and they protested as had their American compatriots a century earlier in the Revolution against England: "No taxation without representation." Indeed, the Hawaiian people were burdened not only with the traditional taxes levied in the states but with several additional taxes not paid by mainlanders. Their sole representation was a single delegate in Congress who was empowered to introduce bills but who had no vote.

Nor were heavy taxes and lack of representation the only inequities dealt the Hawaiian people as U.S. subjects. During World War II Hawaii was placed under martial law, the writ of *habeas corpus* was suspended, and civilians charged with crimes were tried in military courts. These security practices continued long after the threat of invasion had passed, probably because of the same prevailing distrust of Asian-Americans by the whites which had prompted the rise of detention camps for Japanese-Americans on the mainland.

In 1959, both Alaska and Hawaii were admitted to the Union as states, and their people accorded the representation and equal treatment under law denied them for so long. Even today, however, the United States controls other territorial possessions whose people are denied their full rights as U.S. citizens.

Soon after the annexation of Hawaii, America was to record perhaps the most shameful military assault in its history, the Spanish-American War. Cuba was a colony of Spain and in 1894 a Cuban rebellion erupted against the Spanish. American sympathies were on the side of Cuba, which seemed to be fighting for freedom and independence from an autocratic European power. America's major newspapers, such as Joseph Pulitzer's *World* and William Randolph Hearst's *Journal*, in a fierce battle for circulation, created public resentment against Spain by recounting one alleged Spanish atrocity after another. The battle of headlines aroused American readers to a fever pitch.

Sentiments against Spain rose further when the contents of a letter enroute to Spain from the Spanish Minister in Washington were bared by American newsmen. They spoke of President McKinley as an opportunist and a "bidder for the admiration of the crowd." As public furor rose, the Spanish Minister resigned in an effort to quell the outcry, even though his statements about McKinley had been fairly accurate. His resignation, however, did not lessen the American people's readiness for war.

As the Cuban Revolution mounted, President McKinley, concerned with the safety of Americans on that island, dispatched the battleship *Maine* to Havana. Days later, the ship was destroyed in a mysterious explosion, and 260 Americans perished in the disaster. The cause of the *Maine* disaster, though attributed by some historians and muckrakers to William Randolph Hearst and his bid for circulation supremacy in American newspaperdom, has never been confirmed. But the aroused American public immediately charged Spain with the act, though Spain seemed the least likely candidate since she desired to avoid war with the United States at all costs. Nonetheless, anti-Spanish sentiments gripped America. Few considered that the sinking of the *Maine* was more likely the act of a fanatical Cuban group seeking America's support and intervention.

History reveals that McKinley was largely responsible for the war. As war with America loomed, Spain backed down, ordered her forces in Cuba to cease hostilities, and agreed to an armistice with Cuba on the terms prescribed by America. The American minister in Madrid cabled McKinley, "I hope nothing will be done to humiliate Spain." The peace offer reached McKinley before he sent his message to Congress. But the American people clamored for war against Spain, and McKinley acquiesced. The President ignored Spain's offer and asked Congress to declare war on Spain, including only a minor mention of Spain's offer. Thus McKinley led America into a war he could have averted. He ensured his re-election at the cost of American lives in a needless war against a nation which already had capitulated to America's demands. Nor was it a war of glory, for Spain by then was a fifth-rate power, her monarchy weak, her navy reduced to only a few steam-driven wooden hulks. The United States declared war on April 20, 1898, and Spain was forced to reciprocate.

The first fighting erupted in Manila Bay, a Spanish port in the Philippines where America's Admiral Dewey successfully destroyed ten aging and feeble Spanish ships without an American life lost. Few Americans had even heard of the Philippines, but the nation rejoiced at Dewey's easy triumph, unaware of the controversy these islands would soon provoke.

The infantry war that developed in Cuba was not so glorious. The American forces wore wool uniforms in Cuba's torrid heat, carried outmoded weapons, and were commanded by leaders who vied for personal glory. The Spanish troops resisted bravely, but chaos and disorganization riddled the Spanish ranks. As a result, America's victory over the feeble Spanish forces was swift and complete, even despite the U.S. military's gross inefficiency. The majority of Americans who lost their lives in the fray succumbed to typhoid and yellow fever, not enemy fire. Several days after the defeat of the Spanish in Cuba, U.S. forces also occupied Puerto Rico. America's victory had been a cheap one. But problems soon to arise from it would prove costly to the United States.

McKinley thereafter moved to acquire the Philippines from Spain, though the war ostensibly had been fought to "free" Cuba. The nation's anti-imperialists opposed the acquisition, pointing out the obvious contradiction between owning colonies and the spirit of the Declaration of Independence. But the American public generally favored the acquisition, and McKinley again yielded to their will. He supported his action by saying American ownership would bring civilizing advancement to the Filipinos, since they were still largely a "primitive" people, incapable of self-government. In truth, the Filipino people already had established constitutional republican government and, at the time of the American take-over, had elected a president.

Filipino rebels, under the leadership of Aguinaldo, the new president, were enraged by America's impending take-over. They believed America had fought to set them free, and now rebelled against this enslaving Western power. As American occupation forces arrived, the rebel troops launched a furious attack and the Americans countered with massive force. Tales of American rape and torture of the helpless Filipinos filtered back to the United States. Andrew Carnegie wrote to the new American "peace" commissioners, "You seem to have about finished your work of civilizing the Filipinos. About 8,000 of them have been completely civilized and sent to Heaven. . . ." It took three embattled years and 70,000 American troops to finally restore peace to the Philippines. Thereafter, an American civil government was established in the islands without a Filipino vote.

William Howard Taft was the first U.S.-appointed governor of the Philippines. His affable, easy-going personality soon helped assuage the Filipinos' bitterness toward America. But, it was not until 1946, in the wake of a grim atomic war in the Pacific, that the Philippines at last won their long-sought independence. American lobbies were chiefly responsible for the act. Fearing the growing influx of cheap Filipino labor into the United States, American labor unions worked vigorously for termination of America's ownership of the islands. The nation's sugar and tobacco producers also demanded an end to growing Philippine competition and the erection of a firm trade barrier. Thus, powerful American interests succeeded in gaining freedom for the island colony that had been held so long against its will.

The U.S. also established political control over Puerto Rico. Though a civil government was erected, Congress granted neither total self-government nor American citizenship to the Puerto Ricans. Adding insult to their demeaning terms, U.S. officials misspelled Puerto Rico as "Porto Rico" in the declaration delineating her territorial subjugation to America.

Then, although Puerto Rico thereafter was treated as a colony of the United States, import tariffs were levied on its goods. The U.S. Supreme Court upheld the constitutionality of these duties. The Puerto Rican people, shorn of their rights to self-government and representation in Congress despite America's widely-touted democratic traditions, faced the further impasse of an economic trade barrier with the United States.

In 1950, a band of Puerto Rican extremists, seeking to dramatize their nation's desire for independence, attempted without success to assassinate President Harry S. Truman. Thereafter, a group of Puerto Rican nationalists shot and wounded five U.S. Congressmen on the floor of the House of Representatives in Washington, D.C. The resentment and determination of Puerto Rico had made themselves felt. In 1962, it was officially declared a United States commonwealth, with increased autonomy in its own internal affairs.

Though Puerto Rico and the Philippines, both former Spanish possessions, had been annexed by the United States, the Teller Amendment forbade the similar subjugation of Cuba. Problems involving the U.S. arose nonetheless, a result of prejudiced Americans who likened the Cuban people to dirty savages, or "thieving dagoes," as they called them. General Shafter, in charge of U.S. Army forces in Cuba, declared the Cubans "no more fit for self-government than gun-powder is for hell." As Cuban resentment ran high, many American business and political leaders argued for the annexation of Cuba in the interest of heavy American business investment on the island, as well as Cuba's strategic importance politically and economically.

The so-called "independence" granted Cuba by the U.S. did not in actuality make her a sovereign nation. Cuba was forced to make many concessions to the United States, including the granting of U.S. naval bases on her soil, the authorization of intervention by the U.S. in Cuba if her independence were threatened by another power or for protection of "life, and the pursuit of individual liberty," and the promise not to make a treaty with any foreign power that would compromise her independence. This last concession to the U.S. made clear that Cuba was not a free and sovereign nation. After the treaty was signed, hostility against the United States grew in Cuba because of the threat of intervention used by the U.S. to coerce the Cuban government to accept its policies. American investments in Cuba grew rapidly, but without consideration for the welfare of the Cuban people. Americans in Cuba also engendered ill-will by affecting an attitude of superiority toward the able and independent-minded Cuban people, regarding them as "peons" or peasants.

America's self-appointed dominance over Cuba presaged the beginnings of far greater American control extending throughout Latin America. President Theodore Roosevelt declared the United States the "international police power" for the Western Hemisphere. Roosevelt did not want European powers intervening in Pan-America, yet he knew they would if the Latin American nations continued to neglect their debts to European nations as they had in the past. He therefore appointed the U.S. to a policing function to help ensure that her Latin American neighbors would act "responsibly." Though this served to heighten political stability in Latin America, it opened the United States to angry charges of meddling and exploitation. The charges intensified when the Dominican Republic defaulted in its payment to European creditors; the United States took over the Dominican customs service, contributing 55% of the total revenues collected to creditors and the balance to the Dominican government. Though the United States was acting to prevent the interference of European powers in the affairs of the Western Hemisphere, its intervention stirred Latin American resentment, for its neighbors to the south believed it was attempting to control them in a paternalistic manner.

Roosevelt's behavior in the Panama revolution reinforced these Latin resentments and loomed as a large blemish on his Presidential record. Panama was part of Colombia, with whom Roosevelt was unsuccessfully negotiating a treaty to acquire the Panama Canal territory. Colombia was reluctant to sell the territory for the price offered by the United States and was holding out for a higher one. When the Panamanians revolted against Colombia, Roosevelt dispatched the cruiser *Nashville* to Panama to frighten the Colombian forces. Though Panama had revolted against Colombia without success 53 times in the past 57 years, Roosevelt's measure to prevent Colombia's suppression of the uprising guaranteed its success. The victorious Panamanians accepted the Canal treaty with the U.S. on the terms previously rejected by Colombia.

Roosevelt, who had recognized the Republic of Panama only hours after the first fighting had broken out, quickly signed a treaty with Panama guaranteeing America's military might to assure her continuing independence. The U.S. intervention on the side of Panama obviously rewarded the United States well, for Panama drove a far easier bargain than had Colombia. Latin American animosity was inevitable in the wake of Roosevelt's intervention, but was exacerbated by his disparaging references to the Colombians as "dagoes" and his claim that his action against Colombia had been for "the interest of collective civilization." Secretary of War Elihu Root, with regard to the Panama incident, told Roosevelt, "You have shown that you were accused of seduction, and you have conclusively proved that you were guilty of rape." Later, T. R. boasted, "I took the Canal Zone and let Congress debate, and while the debate goes on, the canal does also." Ultimately, in 1921, the United States quietly made amends to Colombia for Roosevelt's actions and paid her $25,000,000 for the "stolen" Panama Canal.

America's interference in the affairs of Latin America continued under President Woodrow Wilson. In 1914 Congress ratified the Bryan-Chamorro Treaty with Nicaragua, making that South American country a protectorate of the United States, and then supported an unpopular dictatorship in power there. Similarly, the U.S. supported the despotic reactionary regime at the helm of the Dominican Republic. When a revolution erupted there in 1916, U.S. Marines were dispatched to occupy the tiny country. They immediately instituted an American military government and imposed stringent censorship upon the nation's press. The Dominican people resented America's invasion and rallied in bitter protest. In 1917 and 1918 they staged repeated revolts against the U.S. occupation forces. Though these uprisings proved futile, the United States at last withdrew its forces and in 1924 permitted a return to civil government in the Dominican Republic. Thus, despite its efforts for over a decade to maintain a pro-American government in power in the tiny country, the United States had failed.

In 1965 U.S. Marines were again dispatched to the Dominican Republic, this time on the pretext of protecting Americans present there during the current rebellion. The real reason for the Marine occupation, however, was that the U.S. Department of State believed Communist forces were dominant in the Dominican rebel movement. It was in the United States' interest to prevent the rise of another Castro Cuba-type government in the Caribbean.

Another target of U.S. intervention was the West Indies republic of Haiti, which over the years had been rocked by one revolution after another. U.S. troops were dispatched to occupy Haiti in 1915, and a puppet president was installed. Soon, Haiti was made a United States protectorate. The Monroe Doctrine was used by Washington to justify the U.S. occupation, extending until 1934. Though America's self-appointed rule of Haiti generated widespread internal improvements there such as new road and school construction, and helped to restore peace, critics charged that the real purpose of America's occupation was to protect her economic interests, while also establishing a military base to guard the major approach to the Panama Canal.

President Wilson's military meddlings in Mexico were even more questionable than those of his in the affairs of other Latin American nations. He twice dispatched U.S. troops into Mexico, twice brought America to the brink of war with her neighbor to the South, and thereby deeply intensified prevailing Mexican anti-American sentiments.

Events beginning in 1911 first prompted Wilson's attention to Mexico. In that year, a liberal coalition overthrew the corrupt dictatorship of Porfirio Diaz, but in turn it was overthrown by the reactionary General Victoriano Huerta. Wilson disliked Huerta and exerted indirect political pressure against him. But the new Mexican dictator drew only strength from Wilson's opposition. President Wilson then declared that America's responsibility was not only to preserve law and order in the Western Hemisphere but to guarantee constitutional democracy within neighboring governments! Since his efforts had failed to tumble Huerta from power, Wilson ordered American troops to invade Mexico through Veracruz. To justify the unwarranted invasion Wilson used America's "indignation" over an erroneous arrest, in a minor incident in Mexico, of several U.S. sailors who were subsequently released. This was hardly justification for war! The Mexicans in Veracruz, whether supporters or enemies of Huerta, fought against the invading U.S. forces vigorously. A total of 400 persons were killed in the battle. Wilson was bombarded with protests from Americans at home, while, in Mexico, even the foes of Huerta denounced Wilson for this gross invasion of their homeland. Mexico and the United States were at the brink of all-out war when Argentina, Brazil and Chile offered to mediate the dispute, thus averting it.

Mexico's democratic forces, led by Venustiano Carranza, finally regained control of the helm of government, but President Wilson continued to meddle blunderingly in Mexico's affairs. When one of Carranza's generals, Pancho Villa, struck out on his own and seized control of Mexico City, Wilson foolishly extended him American support. Villa was merely a powerful *bandito* and the majority of Mexicans remained loyal to the constitutional cause under Carranza. Villa was driven into Northern Mexico. Forced to acknowledge his bumbling error, Wilson swallowed his pride and officially recognized Carranza, whom he should have supported from the beginning.

Thereafter Wilson continued to dictate decisions that proved injurious to America's relations with Mexico. When Pancho Villa led his forces in attacks on settlements across the U.S. border, killing Americans, Wilson dispatched U.S. troops under General Pershing into Mexico to capture him. But the crafty general cleverly evaded the American troops, drawing them further and further into Mexico. This was seen by the Mexicans as a second U.S. invasion of their country, and it aroused such violent anger among them that, in 1916, war between Mexico and America again seemed imminent. Wilson, to his credit, backed down in his plan of aggression, and tempers cooled as the nation's attentions shifted to Europe, where World War I was raging.

America continues to rule over colonies to the present day, including several territorial possessions not yet mentioned here. Guam was acquired in 1898 as one of the prizes of America's victory in the Philippines. Thereafter it was maintained as a military way-station by the U.S. Navy. During World War II Guam was captured by the Japanese and recaptured by the Americans. Today it is the farthest outpost of American territory. Yet the people of Guam have no representation in the U.S. Congress, nor do they vote for the President. They are thereby wholly excluded from democratic participation in the government that dictates and enforces the majority of their laws.

Still another South Pacific territory, Micronesia, composed of the Marshall Islands, the Carolines and Mariana Islands, and encompassing thousands of miles, was given to the United States in a trusteeship by the United Nations. America's use of Micronesia in recent years for the purpose of atomic testing is a blatant misuse of its trust. The atomic explosions there have in no way furthered Micronesia's progress toward independence, while the resulting radiation pollution has endangered the health of the islands' inhabitants. The people of Bikini have seen their homeland made uninhabitable by atomic radiation. Since the Micronesians, according to their culture, traditionally believe that their ancestors and descendants reside in living spirit on their island, the monetary remuneration paid the people of Bikini for the destruction of their island cannot compensate for its loss.

Not once did the U.S. conduct a plebiscite in any territory under acquisition to determine whether its inhabitants desired to be governed by the United States. Only two of these territories have gained full representation in the U.S. Congress, and these only after prolonged and difficult efforts. Indeed, Congress has imposed more severe requirements on these colonies before permitting them to be considered for statehood than on any of the former territories within the contiguous United

States. The economic advancement which has occurred in some of these territories under U.S. rule has been small compensation for their simultaneous surrender of freedom.

American imperialism also continues today in her intervention in the internal affairs of foreign countries. Vietnam, the Dominican Republic and Cuba are but a few recent examples of this imperialist drive, which continues to dictate America's foreign policy.

CHAPTER IX

World War I

The Versailles Treaty, which marked the end of World War I, declared Germany solely responsible for the war. It was unjust, for Germany had not, in fact, triggered the war. In later years historians have assigned a small part of the blame to Germany but charged Serbia, Russia and Austria-Hungary as the major perpetrators. Yet the unjust allegation against Germany in the Versailles Treaty reflected prevailing American public opinion at the time—public opinion which largely continues today. It is unrealistic to believe that a nation as militarily unprepared as Germany in 1914 would purposely start a war. Still, though unprepared for World War I at its onset, Germany fought with determination. The war raged for several years before America entered it. While Germany's role in inciting it was minor, her failure to cultivate America's friendship cost her victory. But America's error was even more serious. The United States allowed itself to be drawn into a costly foreign war which threatened neither its security nor world stature, an involvement which it could have avoided.

When the war in Europe began, the vast majority of the American people favored non-involvement. President Wilson wisely decided to adopt a course of complete neutrality, realizing that neither of the European combatants posed a clear threat to the United States. It was also apparent that neither combatant was the aggressor. But American political sentiments, particularly the pro-English leanings of Wilson and other leaders, made the continuance of total national neutrality difficult. Knowing this, Wilson appealed to the American people to "remain impartial in thought," though many, in fact, continued to favor England in the conflict. U.S. officials never treated the transgressions of Britain as sternly as they did those of Germany, charging the latter with responsibility for any infringement upon American rights while allowing the former wide latitude in her actions. Had Wilson continued in his resolve to stay out of the war and made certain sacrifices to avert involvement, the United States could easily have sailed clear of this senseless and bloody conflict without threat to its security. America's favoritism of Britain largely dictated her needless entry into the war, an act that was to cost her 112,432 lives and leave over 230,000 Americans wounded or disabled.

America's entrance into the war was specifically determined by a series of hostile events at sea, including infringements upon American trade rights and harsh treatment of its citizens aboard passenger ships. Under international law a neutral nation could trade with any belligerent, and the United States was prepared to do so. But Britain, whose powerful navy dominated the Atlantic, officially declared most foreign products bound for German ports, including food, to be "contraband" of war. While international law permitted free trade with belligerents, it specifically barred trade in weapons and munitions. England's ban had the effect of branding all goods bound for Germany as "contraband." She thus forced all neutral ships headed for Germany first to dock in England to be searched by British agents. Often their cargoes were confiscated, without remuneration. Companies based in neutral countries that were found to be trading with Germany were "black-listed" by England and barred from trading within her boundaries. One such blacklist contained the names of 87 American companies.

The English also imposed import quotas on the volume of goods that could be imported into neutral countries. This interference in trade between two wholly neutral countries constituted a gross violation of trading rights. The English sought to justify their violations of international law by stating their import quotas were imperative for national survival in a time of all-out war. Yet this excuse for the disregard of international law could, of course, justify German transgressions as well.

Nonetheless the United States did not demand an end to England's illegal seizures and quotas, though England was so dependent on American aid that she would certainly have bowed to the threat of a United States embargo. America's failure to insist on equitable treatment by England under the provisions of international law amounted to a *de facto* admission of non-neutrality, for Wilson's early proclamation of neutrality was not consonant with later American actions.

England demonstrated ingenuity in her wartime dealings with the United States, for it later became clear she had created the optimum blockade attainable against Germany without causing a *break* with the United States. Throughout this chaotic period when England was running roughshod over America's trading rights, the British propaganda machine was furtively churning out accounts of German war atrocities and spending millions to sway American sentiments even further toward the side of England and the allies.

America's trade with the allies quadrupled in two short years, while her trade with the Central Powers was reduced to a trickle. The allied powers were largely dependent on U.S. materials and supplies. America's loans to the allies soared. Wilson allowed the trade and loans to the allies to continue, despite the pressure they were building for America's entry into the war. Again, in financial matters as in foreign trade, Wilson's seemingly earnest desire for peace was not matched by the motivation toward national policies that would have ensured it.

In 1915 Germany established a blockade of Great Britain and announced that allied vessels entering the waters around the British Isles would be sunk without warning. Wilson retorted hotly that the German aggressors would be held to "strict accountability" in such an event, though he had never held the transgressing English to such a policy. Thereafter he refused to issue a declaration prohibiting Americans from traveling on British ships, virtually assuring that some American travelers would be killed in the announced attacks on British ships by German submarines. The German Navy frequently attacked British ships because they habitually carried munitions. The United States could not expect Germany to halt her attacks on munitions-carrying British ships simply because imprudent Americans were aboard. Indeed German attacks were not only expected, but had been openly *announced in advance* by Germany so that citizens of neutral countries would avoid traveling on British ships, thereby becoming potential and legitimate targets of war. As Secretary of State William Jennings Bryan pointed out,

> A ship carrying contraband should not rely upon passengers to protect her from attack. It would be like putting women and children in front of an army.

Control of civilian travel in wartime had long been an international practice. During the Russo-Japanese War the British government had proclaimed that those of its subjects who chose to travel on ships of belligerent nations could expect no protection from the British government in the event of attack. This stand recognized that even passenger ships often carry munitions in time of war and that this contraband makes them legitimate targets. Thus civilians who traveled on ships carrying war materials did so at their own risk. German submarine commanders attacking British passenger ships in World War I had no way of ensuring the safety of civilians aboard. But President Wilson refused to urge American travelers to avoid taking belligerent ships and declined to make even a mild disavowal of responsibility in such an event, as the British had done ten years earlier. Wilson's silence was to prove critical, for the resulting deaths of Americans at sea ultimately precipitated America's declaration of war. Nor did the United States attempt to end the arming of British merchant vessels by prohibiting their use of American ports. Had America wielded this potent ban, Britain undoubtedly would have discontinued arming her merchant ships, and the loss of American lives would have ended.

The worst sea disaster involving American travelers occurred when the *Lusitania* was sunk in 1915. The British ship, which often flew an American flag as a disguise, carried munitions and explosives. The Germans repeatedly had warned the ship would be attacked. When the *Lusitania* was torpedoed by the Germans, the vast stores of explosives it carried sharply increased the magnitude of the disaster. Among the 1,200 fatalities were 128 Americans. At home, a few U.S. officials called for immediate war on Germany. German protests that fair warning had been issued, even to the extent of German advertisements in U.S. newspapers, did not stave the rising tide of public furor in America. Neutrality diminished in popularity as the rally to war soared. But Wilson refused to be pushed into war, saying,

> There is such a thing as a man being too proud to fight. There is such a thing as a nation being so right that it does not need to convince others by force that it is right.

This wise statement was not accompanied, however, by the adoption of concomitant neutral policies.

Secretary of State Bryan had tried repeatedly to convince President Wilson that the cause of complete neutrality could be served only by keeping Americans off belligerent ships, but the President had refused to heed his urgings. One month after the *Lusitania* incident, as war sentiments mounted, Bryan resigned, citing Wilson's non-neutral practices as the reason. He pointed out that while Wilson held Germany to strict accountability for its actions on the seas, England's flagrant violations of international law were tolerated, even approved. He noted too that America's vast shipments of supplies to England and France during its alleged period of "neutrality" had kept these countries' resistance alive. Without these goods the allies might have been forced to negotiate peace with Germany. Such a settlement early in the war would undoubtedly have produced more equitable terms than those imposed on the totally defeated Germany several years later. Wilson's actions were paradoxical. He showed he desperately wanted to avoid war. Yet he refused to adopt the national and international policies that could have ensured America's continuing neutrality.

Americans were shocked by Germany's torpedoing of the passenger ship *Lusitania*, despite the ample forewarnings and the munitions the ship carried. Yet England's blockade of food shipments from Germany, causing widespread starvation and suffering throughout the continent, aroused no indignation in America. The English blockade caused many more deaths than did the German submarine attack on the *Lusitania* and was as morally reprehensible, but it did not stir American resentment. Thus, one might ask: was America ever, in fact, neutral? The events of the period suggest that her indirect participation in the first three years of World War I might more accurately be termed "non-combatant" on the side of the allies than "neutral."

For a time after the *Lusitania* disaster, German and American tensions eased. Germany agreed to discontinue her attacks upon merchant vessels providing the United States would work for a compromise peace. Germany had no desire to crush England or conquer Europe. The United States pressed for a negotiated settlement, and Germany was willing to accept. But Britain refused. The English assured of a continual flow of American goods and support, replied that they would accept nothing less than total victory.

Midway through World War I, about the time of the U.S. Presidential election of 1916, America seemed more neutral than at any other time in the course of the war. The German attacks on allied ships ceased, although England's illegal and vexing restrictions on neutral trade and shipping continued.

Wilson issued another verbal plea to the belligerent nations urging a compromise peace. But again his plea was refused by the British. Had Wilson only brought economic pressure to bear on Britain at this time she would have been forced to concur with the compromise, for her economy had been stretched to its limits. Thus the war would have been brought to an earlier end, with a more equitable outcome, and America's military intervention would never have occurred. But Wilson refused to bring economic pressure to bear on England.

Then in 1917 Wilson went on record as being unwilling to tolerate the further loss of American lives in the war, even those of Americans aboard armed merchant vessels or munitions-bearing passenger ships. In January of that year, German leaders, incited by the alarming toll of blockade-induced starvation in their country, declared they were ordering the torpedoing of all freighter or passenger ships entering the designated "war zone" circumscribed around Britain, regardless of their country of origin. This action was intended by German leaders as a reprisal against the English blockade. They hoped it would compel England to lift the blockade, thus sparing further thousands of Germany's children and elderly people from starvation. But the German decision was an unfortunate one. Wilson was willing to seek a negotiated settlement between Germany and the allies, but he balked at keeping American ships or American travelers out of British waters, thus paving the way to American deaths in the "war zone" and America's entry into World War I. After several attacks on American ships, Congress declared war on Germany on April 4, 1917, prompted by this new threat to America's "honor" and a long-standing emotional alliance with England.

Wilson knew that Germany posed no direct threat to the United States and that World War I was being fought for no good purpose. He also knew that war would unleash runaway forces of hatred and intolerance in the United States. Yet a decision to enter the war was clearly made by Wilson. He could justify America's declaration of war only by gilding it with idealistic purpose; a new and better world must result from the war, he said. The war must be fought to end all wars.

America's entrance into the war assured an allied victory. America did not win the war and her allies bore the greatest burden of it. But the assurance of her continued support and aid proved just enough added impetus to insure an Allied victory. The United States entered World War I unprepared and her resources were not yet wholly mobilized when the war ended 1½ years later.

Yet, despite the Allied victory, the "Great War," as it was called, yielded a bitter harvest for America. It unleashed vast currents of hatred in America just as Wilson had feared. The U.S. government propaganda machine, under the direction of the mendacious George Creel, whipped Americans into a frenzied hatred of the Germans by portraying them as murderous monsters bent on conquering the world. Creel trained 150,000 men throughout the country to deliver venomous four-minute packaged speeches designed to arouse furor and hatred. American audiences believed the propaganda and supported the growing reign of terror to silence opposition to the war. Americans who declined to buy war bonds were exposed to public ridicule and even assaulted. Mounting anti-German feelings sprang forth across America in ludicrous ways: public school boards outlawed the teaching of the German language, the names of popular German foods were Americanized, and Americans of German descent were persecuted irrespective of their views on the war.

With the ratification of the Espionage Act of 1917, heavy fines and jail sentences were imposed on any American found guilty of aiding the enemy or obstructing the draft. A year later the more insidious Sedition Act was passed and approved by Wilson, making mere criticism of government leaders or their policies sufficient cause for imprisonment. Under this law any persuasive attempt to discourage the sale of war bonds was deemed criminal, as was any effort to "utter, print, or write, or publish any disloyal, profane, scurrilous, or abusive language" about the U.S. government, the Constitution, or the uniform of the army or navy. As a result Eugene Debs was sentenced to ten years in prison for making an anti-war speech, while Hollywood producer Robert Goldstein also received a ten-year sentence for creating a scene showing British Redcoats attacking women and children in a motion picture saga on the American Revolution! Americans were imprisoned merely for criticizing the draft law. Still others were jailed for making critical remarks about organizations such as the YMCA! One woman was sentenced to ten years imprisonment for writing, "I am for the people, and the government is for the profiteers." Clearly the nationwide suppression of free speech far exceeded that which was required for wartime security.

World War I prompted the eruption of the Russian Revolution, a grim event whose consequences have plagued the United States to the present day. Indeed, the ultimate triumph of Communism in the U.S.S.R. and its spread to countless victimized satellite nations are directly attributable to the needless war in Europe, for it was the hardships and hunger in Russia occasioned by the war which shattered Russia's years of economic progress with bloodshed and revolution. Her long ascent to a higher standard of living and a more democratic form of government was halted when she entered World War I, plunging her people into poverty, disease and hunger.

When World War I ended, Wilson's hopes for a just settlement were dashed. England, which had refused to negotiate a peace settlement with Germany during the war, forced the Central Powers to accept the Versailles Treaty. Germany was charged with full responsibility for the war and was ordered to pay "reparations" to the allied nations for their costs of war, including such indirect remunerations as future pensions for military veterans. The total reparations levy upon Germany was 33-billion dollars, a crushing burden which that nation was unable to pay. In contrast to the "Fourteen Points" for a just settlement submitted by Wilson, the treaty was harsh and cruel. The Versailles Treaty, with its unjust charge against Germany and the crushing reparation payments, sowed the first seeds of World War II. In 1949 the United States would again sign a treaty in Paris, declaring that Germany alone was responsible for World War II, an Orwellian misrepresentation of history.

Despite the harsh terms exacted at Versailles, some hope for increased cooperation among world nations was kindled after the war in Wilson's grand design for a league of sovereign nations. The League of Nations, as it was named, was both Wilson's greatest achievement and his most abysmal failure. In the League was vested mankind's only hope of prevention of another world holocaust. Enunciated in the League charter were noble principles and ideals on the brotherhood of man set forth over the centuries by philosophers and saints, but never before made the basis of a political agreement. Wilson failed in his efforts to gain America's membership in the League and this greatly undermined it. In ill health, he resorted to uncharacteristic behavior; he refused to make those compromises with regard to the League that could have ensured America's willing entry. Many in Congress voted against League membership for purely partisan reasons. Still others feared that America, by its entry, might compromise its sovereignty. When a score of years later, World War II broke out, America was faced with the terrible question: Could she have avoided the conflagration by adding her might to the League of Nations?

Woodrow Wilson's performance as President is difficult to evaluate. Though his domestic policies were laudable and far-sighted, his foreign policies remained an enigma. He failed to keep the United States out of World War I despite his ability to do so. He twice sent troops to invade Mexico and committed other transgressions in Latin America. Yet this same man was the "father" of the League of Nations. On the other hand, he failed in his efforts to persuade his own nation to join the League. He was then, in a sense, both the worst and the best of Presidents.

His domestic achievements were substantial. During his administration the Sixteenth Amendment was passed, establishing and authorizing the federal income tax. A short time later was passed the Federal Reserve Act, which restored the nation to a sound banking system. The national currency soon became safe again, yet flexible for the first time since President Jackson had destroyed the banks. Wilson's contributions to progressive reforms also were numerous, but his end achievements, like those of Theodore Roosevelt before him, were limited and disappointed many progressives.

Black Americans profited little from the reform legislation enacted through the efforts of Wilson. The Southern-born President was a firm adherent of segregation. Though in the course of his 1912 election campaign, in a bid to gain black votes, Wilson promised the newly-formed NAACP that if elected he would help elevate American Negroes in every way; once in office he made no effort to do so. Indeed, his dealings actually heightened discrimination against blacks. Wilson also refused to appoint a commission to study Negroes' problems in America, although it was to be privately funded. Many blacks in government civil service lost their jobs, and, under official order, government offices in the Treasury Department and the

Post Office were rigidly segregated, even to their working areas, lunchrooms and restrooms. Those who protested this sudden policy of enforced discrimination were terminated. When Wilson came under attack he refused to repudiate this segregation policy. Even today it looms as a regrettable mark against the record of this otherwise humanitarian President.

Wilson's tenure ended on a sad note. During his last months in office he was physically and mentally incapacitated, incompetent to perform the total duties of his office. In September, 1919, he suffered a severe stroke which resulted in partial paralysis to his left side. For the next several months he withdrew from his active role in the affairs of state. His wife, Edith, assumed much of the responsibility of the chief executive. The nation drifted leaderless through Wilson's final months in office.

Immediately after the end of World War I America withdrew into isolationism, essentially severing its diplomatic ties with the world. Thereafter the United States steadfastly refused to participate actively in world affairs until the outbreak of World War II. The "great war to end all wars" had been a regrettable tragedy that most Americans wanted to forget. Yet, during the decades ahead, a series of events occurred which made the Great War seem a remote and distant memory.

CHAPTER X

Interbellum

The 1920's ushered in a decade of "normalcy" in America, a term coined by President Warren G. Harding to denote the nation's return to relative social and economic peacetime stability after the tension, shortages and unrest accompanying World War I. Despite this "normalcy," the shortlived period was to witness mounting national tensions, made manifest in America's growing symptoms of xenophobia (irrational fear and hatred of foreigners), rampant materialism, political corruption, prohibition, and ultimately, the Great Depression of 1929. Though the dazzling prosperity and giddy exuberance of the "Roaring Twenties" in America were overshadowed by the nation's growing internal disillusionment and despair, both paled in comparison to the intensity of the Great Depression, an event so severe it wrought total revision in the U.S. economy.

These years of national unrest had their basis in World War I. The American people, living in the shadow of this "war to end all wars," were seeking desperately to escape its widely-felt influence. Many were disenchanted with the idealism that had been championed by Woodrow Wilson and used to guide national policy for years. Others were aware America had made a grave mistake in entering the war. Nearly all wanted a return to the "good life." Harding had promised in his vigorous campaign a return to "normalcy." Americans clearly needed a major diversion to take their minds off the war. In the brief interbellum years some Americans achieved this through dedicated cynicism or rampant materialism, and others, in a fervid quest for individuality or national isolationism.

Compounding the tensions accompanying America's peacetime transition was the failure of its leaders to redirect its wartime organization to productive peacetime purposes. During the war the nation's leaders had successfully mustered vast, cohesive public action in cities, towns and communities across America to achieve rapid mobilization. But at war's end, instead of redirecting this grass-roots fervor and organization toward the solution of America's domestic peacetime problems, national leaders turned their attentions largely to political and personal pursuits and wholly rejected the potential the war organization had fostered.

These same leaders generally adopted a *laissez faire* attitude toward the nation's peacetime needs. Most voters were content with this relaxation of leadership as popular attention focussed on thrill-seeking ribaldry and a pronounced departure from the Victorian morality which had guided earlier eras.

America's young were at the forefront of these "ballyhoo" years, rejecting the conservative morality of their predecessors in favor of conspicuous amorality and the growing love of fads. Once relatively unimportant events, such as championship prize-fights, seized the nation's interest and enthusiasm. Though Charles Lindbergh's non-stop flight across the Atlantic was actually but one of many such flights achieved by American aviators, it captured the attention of the entire nation. Lindbergh and other marathon fliers suddenly became national heroes in the onslaught of ticker-tape parades, worldwide newsreel coverage, and Presidential citations. Soon every variety of ludicrous fad was seizing the imagination of millions.

The nation's morality, especially among its young, was also changing. Although Freud's real posture was a highly moral one, his psychological writings as they spread to America sharply revised the nation's attitudes toward sex, particularly among intellectuals and college students. This changing attitude gained momentum from the privacy and mobility of the new "sin" machine—the automobile. The "liberated woman" began to emerge—in revealing dresses, bobbed hair, flamboyant make-up, with cigarette in hand, and participating in night rides to secluded spots. America's divorce rate soared and a record thousands of infants were born out of wedlock as traditional mores gave way to the "new morality."

Despite the fun-filled picture often drawn of the Roaring Twenties, underneath it was a grimly uncertain era of widespread public fear and anxiety. One prevalent worry among many Americans was that of the threat of Communism. The Russian Revolution did much to kindle American fears of a Communist take-over. The revolution in Russia had been successfully fomented by only a small band of radicals. When these Marxists announced that their intention was to incite worldwide revolution, many Americans grew understandably fearful. Some erroneously linked the increase of unionism and strikes after World War I to this Communist threat and feared the nation was on the verge of violent revolution. What these people did not realize was that the very progress made by American workers through labor unions was helping to dispel a major reason in America for possible revolution. Too, the actions of a number of anarchists heightened America's fears of Communist take-over when they made attempts on the lives of national leaders by sending them bombs in the mail. In another rash of incidents, explosives were detonated in several major cities. The perpetrators, when apprehended, often proved to be foreign anarchists. These events led eventually to the great "Red Scare" and witchhunt of 1920, an unfortunate epic similar in its frenzy to Senator McCarthy's "Redherring" hearings three decades later.

Several events of the 1920's illustrate the extent to which fear and hatred gripped the American people. An accused murderer on trial in Indiana was acquitted by a jury within two minutes because testimony revealed his victim had shouted, "To hell with the United States." The New York State Assembly expelled five elected assemblymen because they belonged to the Socialist Party. This act disenfranchised the citizens of their respective districts, depriving them of their representation in the state assembly simply because a majority of legislators condemned the beliefs of the representatives who had been elected.

A growing number of demands poured into Washington from

all parts of the nation for legislation to suppress the activities of all radicals. The federal government soon responded to public pressure. The resulting great "witchhunt" of 1920 was directed by A. Mitchell Palmer, attorney general under Woodrow Wilson. Responding to the public uproar and the desire for public popularity in the event he decided to campaign for future elective office, Palmer ordered the arrests of 650 working aliens nationwide. Evidence was sufficient to deport only 43 of those arrested. Though no evidence could be found to support the arrest of the remaining aliens, public reaction to the wholesale imprisonments was favorable across the nation. Eyeing the 1920 Democratic Presidential nomination, Palmer soon conceived an even larger-scale plan of wholesale arrests.

On January 2, 1920, this "ground plan" was implemented by Palmer in 33 cities across the nation. He had gathered 3,000 arrest warrants from judges at the local levels. His agents, assisted by police and vigilantes, stormed houses and meeting places in the series of famous "Palmer raids." Persons were seized and arrested at meetings with no provision for notifying their families of their whereabouts. Some 6,000 were imprisoned, many being held without evidence. Often the accused were held incommunicado for weeks while police searched frantically for evidence, and their families worried. Of the 6,000 seized in the Palmer raids, only 556 were subject to deportation. Prominent lawyers, as well as several leading magazines, came forth to denounce Palmer's extreme tactics and the suppression of civil liberties occasioned by the raids. The realization spread quickly that the civil liberties of all Americans would be jeopardized if Palmer's raids were allowed to continue. As numerous magazine articles made clear that many innocent victims were being arrested, the feverish national fear of Communist takeover soon reversed itself into a scathing attack on the tactics of Attorney General Palmer. The "Red Scare" ended as quickly as it had begun, draining Palmer's public support. As the fearful overreaction subsided, Palmer seemed a gross and ridiculous figure to the public that had so recently supported him.

Federal agents continued to pursue the elusive Communists, but in less obtrusive ways. The Ku Klux Klan sustained its reign of terror, greatly increasing its strength in the post-war years. Minorities, such as Roman Catholics, Jews and blacks, continued to face discrimination. Nor did America's widespread xenophobia subside with the termination of the "Red Scare." One manifestation of this intolerance toward aliens was the harsh and discriminatory laws governing quotas. In enacting these laws, Congress abandoned the principle of the "melting pot" and undermined the once-noble ideal of a land of opportunity "for all." In its Immigration Acts of 1924 and 1929, it instead committed itself to the preservation of a dominantly white Anglo-Saxon population. Asians were barred from permanent admission to the U.S. and naturalization as citizens, while immigrants from many other nations were subjected to national quota restrictions. Those from Western European countries, however, such as England, were deemed admissible virtually without limit on their numbers.

The Japanese were especially resentful of the blatant discrimination apparent in the restrictions on all Asians. But the nations of Southern Europe also felt the brunt of America's discrimination in the sharply reduced U.S. immigration quotas enforced on their countrymen. While England was accorded an annual quota of 65,000, Greece was allotted only 308 immigrants. Yet the demand for immigration proved to be in quite the opposite proportions: while English immigrants filled less than 10% of their U.S. quota between 1931 and 1939, only a tiny fraction of the vast number of Greeks desiring to immigrate to the United States ever were allowed to do so. In 1920, the number of immigrants admitted into the United States was 805,000; in 1930, fewer than 150,000 entered. Even if by the decision of federal policy-makers America was no longer to be open as a land of opportunity for all, it would have been fairer to set a universal limit on the number of immigrants admitted from all countries rather than permit the inequitable quotas which were enacted. America in effect had announced to the world that it was closing its doors to all except white Anglo-Saxons.

Not until 1943 were Chinese again allowed to enter the United States. Filipinos, though residents of a U.S. protectorate, were not allowed admission and residence in the U.S. until 1946. Then, in 1952, revision of the immigration laws governing Asian peoples permitted them entry into the United States on the basis of small racial, rather than national, quotas. Not until 1965 were these and other inequities within the United States immigration code eliminated by the passage of the Immigration Act, thus ending more than 30 years of anti-alien sentiment in America wrought in the fear and anxiety of the 1920's.

America's attitude toward foreigners and foreign relations in the 1920's was illustrated by its withdrawal into isolationism soon after World War I. The League of Nations thereafter not only was ignored by the United States, but was treated with contempt by it. State Department officials even refused to answer letters from the League Secretariat. Though the United States signed a number of international treaties with other major powers during this period, they were mere pacts of friendship and contained no provisions for their enforcement. America would make no world commitments beyond mere words. In the Kellogg-Briand pact of 1928, all the signatories agreed to never again take up arms in war. Fifteen nations signed this vague document, which contained idealistic words but no statement of a realistic method to guarantee that the nations signing it would abide by its terms. That same year the United States Senate ratified the treaty by a vote of 85 to 1. Most Americans viewed it as a milestone in man's centuries-old quest for peace. America's isolationist attitude during the 1920's had a positive effect in Latin America, for America at last declined to act on her "right" to intervene in the affairs of Western Hemisphere nations, a practice which she had pursued for several previous decades. Yet the overall effect of America's withdrawal from foreign involvements caused her to decline to provide sorely needed assistance to other nations, and thus to serve as a positive influence on the course of world events.

As U.S. leaders withdrew from participation in world affairs they also lapsed in their control of the nation's domestic affairs.

Presiding over this non-governing government of the early 1920's was Warren G. Harding, a man who looked like a distinguished statesman, yet had few statesmanlike qualities. The electorate's choice of Harding for its return to "normalcy" was indeed appropriate, for he embodied what the people desired most in the wake of the vexing World War—a placid, do-nothing government.

Harding was strikingly handsome, the epitome of dignity and poise. He also was the friendliest man ever to occupy the White House. Despite these qualities and his undeniable assets, he also brought to office a number of liabilities. Harding was not very intelligent; his comprehension was vague, often fuzzy, and bewildered by the complex demands of high office. He appointed several astute advisors, including Mellon, Hoover and Hughes, but rarely understood their counsel and appeared confused when confronted with opposing viewpoints on an issue. Not even President Grant had been as ill-suited for the enormous tasks of the Presidency. Harding admitted his ineptness, declaring he did not know where to turn for the answers to critical questions. He was wholly dependent on the advice of subordinates and those he chiefly relied on were not of the caliber of Herbert Hoover, for Harding also was not a consistently good judge of men. He appointed old cronies to high office, often incompetent and unscrupulous men. Among these were Attorney General Harry M. Daugherty, Secretary of the Interior Albert B. Fall, Director of the U.S. Mint Ed Scobey, and Veterans Bureau Director Charles Forbes. All were close personal friends of Harding and shared his penchant for drinking, gambling, and comely women. These men possessed no notable qualifications for the high federal posts to which they were appointed. Ultimately they were to plunge Harding's administration into greater corruption than had Grant's advisors during his Presidency.

As Director of the Veterans Bureau, Charles Forbes siphoned millions allocated for the construction of Veterans Hospitals into his own pocket. When his thefts were exposed he fled to Europe. On his ultimate return to the United States he was tried and sentenced to a two-year jail term. This was a mild rebuke for the millions of dollars Forbes had filched from the Veterans Bureau in two short years.

Harry Daugherty was awarded the post of U.S. Attorney General for his devoted performance as Harding's presidential campaign manager. While in office he presided as leader of the "Ohio Gang," which amassed great wealth during the prohibition period by selling protection to bootleggers and from payoffs secured for awarding government contracts and public office to a favored few. So flagrant was Daugherty's unscrupulousness that he sold pardons and paroles to imprisoned criminals while serving as U.S. Attorney General! When Daugherty's nefarious dealings were bared after Harding's death, the former Attorney General managed successfully to avoid punishment.

Secretary of the Interior Albert Fall received at least $400,000 in confidential payoffs for leasing federal lands to oil companies. Those that secured land leases in Teapot Dome, Wyoming and Elk Hills, California expected to net several hundred million dollars in profit, but the leases were cancelled after Harding's death when Senate investigators exposed Fall's dealings. Fall received a one-year sentence and was fined $100,000, thus netting a sizeable profit from his nefarious deeds. Scandals involving other lower-level Harding appointees were bared after his death. Several of those implicated chose suicide over the shame of public exposure.

Even Harding's death was surrounded by questionable circumstances, though the cause remains uncertain to this day. Some evidence points to suicide while a case has also been made for murder by his wife and physician. The official report stated Harding had suffered ptomaine poisoning as a result of eating tainted crab meat during a return boat trip from Alaska. None of the others aboard were stricken, however. Even more striking was that crab meat was not listed among the provisions in the steward's pantry. Harding's condition was reported to be rapidly improving when, suddenly, he died. No autopsy was ordered. Perhaps the real cause of his death will forever go unrecorded. Adding to its mysteriousness were the deaths soon afterward of a startling number of persons closely linked to

Harding, including his wife, his physician and several key men within his cabinet, nearly all of whom had been party to various corrupt dealings while in office.

Whereas Woodrow Wilson had spurred America to strive for peace and ideals, Warren Harding had promised the war-weary nation a respite and a return to "normalcy." He was a simple, earthly man whose commonness deeply appealed to the people of his day. How earthy he was was revealed later in a book written after his death by Harding's mistress, Nan Britton, who noted that their rendezvous occurred even in such unlikely places as a White House broom closet. Yet Harding's immense popularity up to the time of his death proved he fulfilled the desires of the majority of the electorate.

His successor, Calvin Coolidge, excelled him only slightly as an effective President. Wrote Walter Lippman,

> Mr. Coolidge's genius for inactivity is developed to a very high point . . . It is a grim, determined, alert inactivity, which keeps Mr. Coolidge occupied constantly.

Coolidge refrained from exerting strong leadership, and Congress thus ran the country during his term in office. Like Harding, Coolidge maintained his far-reaching popularity by being the very quintessence of a do-nothing leader, a quality which the American people seemed to desire in the post-war years.

Perhaps the most publicized product of the 1920's was America's "noble experiment," prohibition. The ratification of the Eighteenth Amendment ended the sale of all alcoholic beverages within the United States, including beer and wine. Passage of the amendment was aided by the prevailing xenophobia of the day, as Americans linked aliens with certain beverages, such as Germans with beer and Italians with wine. The association of alcohol with these disfavored foreign minorities added momentum to the program of America's social idealists, who, by prohibition, hoped to remake the world. Their "noble experiment" had some positive results: cases of alcoholism fell off sharply, as did arrests for public drunkenness.

Yet the negative aspects of Prohibition also are well-remembered: the underworld gained strength and wealth as the chief purveyor of illegal liquor, contempt for the law became manifest even among previously law-abiding citizens, and hypocrisy prevailed in political office. Everywhere flagrant violations of prohibition occurred. President Harding openly served liquor in the White House, while speakeasies flourished across the nation, usually under the protection of local police. Utter disregard for the Volstead Act, which enforced prohibition, was evident everywhere. "Wets," as those opposing prohibition were called, contended that the widespread disregard of the Eighteenth Amendment would soon erupt into contempt for all law and that general lawlessness thereby would be inevitable. Wets and drys argued vehemently over the question of prohibition. One such argument centered around whether alcohol consumption had risen or declined since the onset of prohibition. While the consumption of alcohol undoubtedly was lower than at pre-prohibition levels, since alcohol consumption had been outlawed altogether, this revealed only too plainly the failure of the Volstead Act to end such consumption and the willingness of countless Americans to break the law.

Federal leaders came to realize at last that the negative results of prohibition far outweighed the positive, and the law could not be effectively enforced. But few would speak out against it, fearful of losing conservative votes. Because politicians equivocated at such length on the issue, never directly stating their opposition, prohibition was not repealed until 1933.

The 1920's, romantic, yet fraught with lawlessness and unrest, ended with the Great Depression of 1929. The minor depression which was felt throughout America just after World War I presaged the critical one a decade later. The former resulted when military veterans were suddenly cast into the labor market without any government efforts to promote or create jobs to accommodate the surge. Widespread unemployment was the result. As wartime economic controls were rapidly released, no provisions had been made to take up the slack in the economy. Rapid inflation was followed by falling prices and depression in 1920.

While the United States had suffered many prior economic depressions, none more intensely shook the faith of Americans in their economic system than the Great Depression of 1929. Ultimately it was to affect the entire world, as no industrialized nation was able to escape the repercussions of America's crumbling economy. The Great Depression, as well as the numerous declines of the 1800's, present a continuing challenge to uncontrolled capitalism which has never been answered: are unemployment and depression inherent in the capitalistic economy? Indeed, whether the American economic system can maintain prosperity and full employment in peacetime remains a crucial issue. During the Great Depression Franklin D. Roosevelt installed centralized government controls. Since then the federal government has enacted measures to increasingly control the nation's economy. As individual initiative and free competition became more and more circumscribed over the years, the American system has moved in the direction of the planned economy envisioned in other economic systems. The Great Depression presented a challenge which pure capitalism could not meet, and unfettered free enterprise was abandoned.

The onset of the Great Depression of 1929 came without warning to many Americans. Stocks declined suddenly, and their drop caused alarmed Americans to lose faith in the economy; the market plunged downward, pulling with it the entire nation. Many people, fearful that hard times were ahead, saved all the money they could, buying only necessities. The resulting fall-off in sales forced many companies to lay off workers. As unemployment rose the economy's downward spiral hastened. Thus underconsumption and unemployment, each feeding the other, grew to catastrophic proportions. The ranks of unemployed swelled to some 13-million, while national income fell from $80-billion to $50-billion in a three-year period. At a time when the hungry roamed the countryside and some in the cities starved to death, food prices fell so low that many farmers chose to burn their crops rather than take them to market!

President Herbert Hoover mapped many programs to check the nation's economic plunge, but his plans were generally too late or not comprehensive enough to meet the immensity of the problem. Hoover relied upon the good-will of businessmen to reverse the plight of the nation, but this proved a dismal failure. The President rigidly adhered to conventional economic principles that could not serve in a time of crisis when sweeping reforms were direly needed. His staunch adherence to a balanced budget at the height of the Depression greatly curtailed his ability to stimulate recovery. He refused, on Constitutional grounds, to allow federal funds to be used for public welfare, though he regarded federal aid to businessmen as Constitutional and approved such assistance, chiefly in the form of loans. Hoover believed the distressed economy was at its low point and that new prosperity waited just around the corner. But his pronouncement proved wrong as the economy grew steadily bleaker. In addition, he relied too heavily for solutions on state and local governments, rather than acknowledging that the immensity of the crisis required the full power and resources of the federal government to shape an adequate solution. Throughout his four years in office Hoover remained inflexible and refused to experiment or innovate in the time of America's darkest economic hour.

Franklin D. Roosevelt's intervention came just in time, for in 1932 a revolution seemed imminent. Many of the nation's farmers seethed with discontent, some barely able to make a living and thousands more having lost their hard-earned land. Millions in the cities were unemployed. Thousands talked of revolution as the only course. Though this was rarely inspired by Marxist ideas, many were impressed with the economic stability and growth of Russia resulting from its revolution a scant 15 years earlier.

Roosevelt came to the Presidency as the last hope of a nation on the verge of crumbling. FDR is said to have stated that, if his relief measures failed, he might be the last President of the United States. Hoover's failure had been in his inability to imbue the nation with spirit, to restore the people's confidence in the economy and lead them out of despair. Franklin Roosevelt's success stemmed not so much from his economic policies, which were often barely more effective than Hoover's, but from his ability to rally the people to action and to strike new hope in the beleaguered nation.

Roosevelt lacked a concrete plan of action, but he knew the federal government must act swiftly to check the economic blight. He saw experimentation as the only course, lacking as he did, definite answers. FDR may not have comprehended the causes of the Depression any more than had Hoover, nor did his plans ever completely curb it, but he did spark the nation's hope and enacted measures which partially reversed the plunge. Slowly the plummeting economy began to level off.

FDR's famous first 100 days saw far-reaching measures enacted, such as the creation of the Tennessee Valley Authority, the National Industrial Recovery Act, the Civilian Conservation Corps, and the Agricultural Adjustment Administration. Though the move toward recovery spurred by the Hundred Days did not continue for long, the nation again was imbued with an aura of optimism. Roosevelt himself seemed changed by those one-hundred days from a politician of charm to a leader of dynamic aggressiveness.

Following, in 1935, were the second Hundred Days, the so-called "Second New Deal." A spate of laws were passed, chiefly aimed at helping labor rather than business which by this time was turning against Roosevelt's liberal policies. One of these measures, FDR's Wealth Tax Act, levied heavy taxes on the upper class to secure revenue for government operation and to help redistribute the nation's wealth.

The combined legislation enacted during the two "Hundred Day" periods comprised a bold, large-scale program toward establishing a planned economy in the United States. Herbert Hoover branded the New Deal "the most stupendous invasion of the whole spirit of liberty that the nation has witnessed." Indeed, the New Deal regulated the national economy to an extent unbelievable a decade earlier. Only Communists and Socialists had conceived of the possibility of such comprehensive planning and control prior to the Great Depression.

In drafting his programs FDR acted upon the Keynesian theory, an economic hypothesis which he never believed nor even fully understood. But the sheer exigencies of the Depression and the measures needed to curtail it forced him to spend more than the federal government was collecting in revenues. Thus he inadvertently adopted the Keynesian strategy though he had little faith in it. From 1933 to 1937 the business cycle rose slowly. In 1937 FDR, not cognizant of the importance of government spending to stimulate recovery, cut back on relief programs. A new decline began. He reacted to this new recession much as Hoover might have done, maintaining that the slump would reverse itself with time and patience. Roosevelt continued inactive and indecisive for almost a year, while the economy drifted further downward. At last he acquiesced and committed the federal government to increased spending, whereupon the decline ended.

In 1938 FDR shifted his attention from the decade-long depression to foreign affairs. When war erupted in Europe the following year the American economy soared, stimulated by export sales to the democratic nations of Europe. When the U.S. entered the war in 1941, its economy had surpassed its peak level of 1929. FDR's policies had helped bring the nation slowly out of its decline, but the war provided the real impetus needed to revitalize the American economy. Again, it could be seen that modern capitalism flourishes best in times of massive mobilization and military spending.

The policies effected by Franklin D. Roosevelt have engendered two lasting phenomena in America: (1) the permanent curb on the freedom of private business, and (2) recognition of the federal government as the dominant controller of the nation's economy and the sole source for averting or rectifying recessions and depressions alike. The American economy, drastically altered by the crisis and cures of its ten Depression years, will never again operate in the flexibility and unrestraint of the free capitalism of 1929.

CHAPTER XI

World War II

The Second World War often is considered the one war in U.S. history the wisdom and morality of which are unquestionable. Even historians who view other American wars with critical embarrassment acclaim World War II in an uncritical way. At its outset, although American intervention seemed unlikely, the pros and cons of such intervention were hotly debated. But once the decision to intervene was made, only the pro-war arguments were remembered.

Though World War II may have seemed necessary at the time, in retrospect it was far from successful, and many of the problems the U.S. faces today stem from it. In its aftermath Russia rose to become the world's second greatest power, while the concurrent decline of Europe left the U.S.'s major adversary to dominate two continents, unopposed by any nation rivaling her might. Chiang Kai-Shek's forces in China were so weakened by the war that Communist takeover was possible, leaving a large portion of the world's population under a system which many Americans consider more obnoxious than Fascism. Ironically, the U.S. fought alongside Russia, which invaded innocent countries with tactics similar to those of Germany and Japan. Soviet invasion of Finland is a case in point. What of the Soviet seizure of Bukovina and part of Moldavia, and her proposal to take over the Balkans and Turkey? It is often said, though not proven, that Hitler was bent on a course of world mastery, yet this has been true too of world Communism. It has been argued that, had the United States not entered the war when she did, she would have been left to face Nazism alone, the sole contender remaining against this terrible totalitarian menace. Yet this too remains unproven.

In retrospect, perhaps those isolationists (including Harry Truman in 1941) who advised letting Germany and Russia battle it out with each other, thereby exhausting their mutual strength, were not mistaken. It may be that America's entrance into the war saved Western Europe from Communist takeover. Yet Russia emerged with vast natural resources and twice the population of pre-war Germany to dominate Europe and Asia. If neutrality in the face of Hitler's invasions was unfortunate, what of America's commitments to Russia at Yalta and Teheran? And if the U.S. entered the war to fight totalitarianism which strangled human freedoms, why did she ally with a Soviet dictatorship which murdered its own citizens in Stalin's bloody purges? Few of the reasons most cited for America's entry into World War II stand up to critical examination.

The events of the 1930's leading up to World War II are often misrepresented. England and France did not stand by helplessly while Hitler overran Czechoslovakia and Austria. Rather, the two Western democracies looked on these seizures approvingly, hoping that, as Germany grew strong and moved eastward, she eventually would confront and defeat the most hated enemy of all, the Bolsheviks. England's plan under Chamberlain was to allow Hitler, a staunch anti-Communist, to fortify Germany and expand eastward until he clashed with Russia and defeated the Reds for whom England had only contempt. Nor did Chamberlain sit idly by while Hitler stormed Czechoslovakia; he took an active part in her dismemberment. Chamberlain urged the Prague government to accept Hitler's demand for the secession of the Sudetenland, a German-speaking area of Czechoslovakia, and later, at the Munich conference of 1938, both England and France approved Hitler's takeover.

England still was the leading European power and moved in the most calculating ways to retain her power. On his part, Hitler desired a large area of Eastern Europe as "living space" for German-speaking peoples, but entertained little thought, at the time, of fighting the Western European countries.

As this balance-of-power interplay heightened in Western Europe, a startling event occurred: Germany and Russia announced the signing of a mutual non-aggression pact, which consolidated the two prior arch-enemies into allies. England was stunned. She had believed Nazi Germany to be almost a tool of her ambitions. Now Hitler had struck out on his own, and worse, had signed a treaty with the hated U.S.S.R., a treaty which threatened England's hegemony. So long as England could count on Russia's and Germany's enmity, her dominant stature was assured. But now the new allies posed a dangerous threat to British power and cast a wholly new light on any further German expansion.

Prior to the German-Russian *detente,* England had been quite willing to let Germany seize Poland, knowing this would provide the Nazis the needed invasion route to Russia. Just as the British had intervened in Prague to help Germany acquire the Sudetenland, so they also had been instrumental in helping the Nazis acquire the Rhineland. As late as March, 1939, Stalin complained that the European powers and the United States were inciting Hitler to march on Russia.

When the German-Russian rapprochement came in 1939, England quickly improvised a treaty with Poland, not because she finally saw the only way to stop Hitler was to confront him, but in an attempt to curb growing German power. It had no desire to go to war with Germany nor did Germany want to fight the British. Hitler demanded the free city of Danzig from the Poles and an extra-territorial railway through Poland to link Prussia with the rest of Germany. England urged the Poles to make these concessions lest war result, but Poland stubbornly refused to be a pawn in the power struggle and actually believed she stood a good chance in a fight with Germany. Thus, in 1939, Poland denied concessions that might have saved her from German attack. When Hitler finally invaded Poland, Chamberlain moved to make peace with Germany, but English opinion objected strongly. The House of Commons forced the elderly Prime Minister to declare war.

The Nazi blitzkrieg subjugated Poland in only three weeks. Thereafter, in October, 1939, Hitler attempted to make peace with Britain, but to no avail. Britain could no longer hope for a German attack on the Bolsheviks, nor could she negate the pact made so recently with Poland.

It is noteworthy that both the United States and Russia declared themselves neutral as France and Britain joined in war against Germany. Also significant was Russia's part in the division of Poland, like a scavaging hyena, once Germany had made the kill. Soviet occupation of Eastern Poland had been prearranged in an earlier pact with Germany. Russia loomed guilty of the subjugation of Poland as was Germany, which, once she had conquered the Poles whom she regarded as inferior beings, she began to exterminate.

As the war intensified Germany unleashed greater shows of military might than anyone had anticipated. In fact, it would ultimately take the world's three greatest powers to defeat a Germany that had no powerful European allies. In 1939 Germany had no intention of carrying her military aggression beyond the borders of Poland; the combined armies of France and England were larger than her own. Yet, as the war went on, the qualitative superiority of the German forces began to be obvious. France fell quickly and it soon appeared that England would be no match for her. Only the Channel saved Britain from Germany's devastating land-war strategies, and it seemed fated that Britain would eventually fall to the Luftwaffe. Though Franklin D. Roosevelt issued aid to England and sought to help her in every way, the American people stood firmly against United States involvement in the war. But it was not America that was to save England. Ironically, it was Britain's old adversary, Russia, and Hitler's grave miscalculation —that of invading the U.S.S.R.—in 1940.

The new Russian front took the pressure off of England at a time when her defenses were faring badly. But Hitler's attack on the U.S.S.R., thought by many to be no match for Germany, proved to be his greatest blunder. Though the United States, drawn into the war in 1941, claimed major credit for Hitler's defeat, it was the Russians who bore the brunt of the fighting, suffered the heaviest casualties, and carried out the central role in Germany's defeat.

Germany's attack on Russia only one year after signing their mutual non-aggression pact is often cited as evidence of Hitler's utter ruthlessness. There is no denying that Hitler was ruthless, but in the case of the Russian invasion that was not the entire story. The Soviets had already violated the pact by seizing Bukovina and part of Moldavia in June, 1940, although these territories lay beyond the demarcation line for Russian claims. In 1940 the Soviets massed troops along the German border, long before any German troop action. That same year the Communists figured importantly in the overthrow of the Yugoslav government. And the Soviets invaded Finland, justified only by the desire to gain a strategic base from which to fight Hitler effectively at a later date.

In the light of these Soviet provocations, Germany's attack on Russia might even be viewed as a preventative one. As these two great totalitarian powers did battle, the world watched, its democracies hoping to profit from their mutual devastation. But which of the two was more justified? Both had invaded innocent lands, both had demonstrated equal ruthlessness, and both were foes of free and democratic government. Harry Truman was serious when he stated that Russia, though an American ally, was the greater threat of the two, and that America should ally with Germany should the Russian forces begin to triumph. Former President Hoover declared it "a mockery" to pretend the war was a struggle for democracy over despotism, while Senator Taft asserted,

> The victory of Communism in the world would be far more dangerous to the United States than a victory of Fascism.

Britain's original aim had been for a strong Germany to attack and defeat Russia. When the Nazis attacked the U.S.S.R., it was believed the Soviets would soon succumb, fulfilling at least that part of the Britains' early plan. England, however, now was fighting to defeat a Germany far stronger than she had anticipated. World historians have largely neglected to note the key role of England's ambitions in triggering the war.

The measures by which Franklin Delano Roosevelt brought America into the war, starting with his directives against Japan's aggressive policies in the Orient, also warrant note. The Japanese offered several explanations for their aggression. Having a vast population confined to a very small land area, they needed room for expansion, room that could be gained only by force. Japan also sought, through territorial acquisitions, to strengthen her position against her traditional arch-enemy, Russia. The earlier acquisition of colonies by force by the Western powers exemplified to the Japanese how they might enlarge their land holdings. Further, their overflow population could not emigrate easily, barred by quota restrictions in such countries as Australia and the United States. When Japan attempted to inject a racial equality clause in the League of Nations covenant, the Western democracies defeated her efforts, and discriminatory immigration policies continued in many countries. This heightened Japan's resentment and gave strength to the militant faction which ultimately gained control of the government.

Throughout her aggressive build-up and even after signing a pact with the Axis powers, Japan hoped—however unrealistically—to continue her good relationship with the United States, relying almost completely as she did on American industrial resources, such as oil and steel. In 1940 Japan asked a resident Catholic bishop to travel to Washington, D. C. and express her desire to negotiate a peace treaty with the United States. Anxious to secure this treaty so vital to their interests, the Japanese implied willingness to: (1) nullify their earlier pact with the Axis, and (2) recall their occupation forces from China, thus helping to restore its political integrity. Japan also proposed that negotiations with the United States on other important issues ensue.

Rather than following up this peace bid, the Roosevelt administration responded that it would take the matter "under advisement": that is, do nothing. Later administration talks with Nomura, the Japanese ambassador to the United States, revealed that Japan was no longer willing to offer such concessions.

Hopes for a potential treaty between Japan and the United States were further dampened by the signing of the Atlantic Charter by Roosevelt and Churchill in August, 1941. Roosevelt agreed with Britain's suggestion that America be ready to repel a possible Japanese thrust anywhere in the Pacific area against the British colonies or Russia. Yet he did not announce this decision to the American public, fearful their "ignorance" of strategic defense might cause them to condemn this preparedness policy, which was bringing America closer to war. Thus, publicly Roosevelt continued the pretense of attempting reconciliation with Japan, while privately his administration took a hard-line stand that made America's entry into the war almost inevitable. Japan's proposal of a meeting between her Prince Konoe and F.D.R. was rejected by Washington. This proved a serious blow to Japan's peace efforts, and the Japanese began to prepare militarily for the clash with the United States that now seemed imminent.

It is difficult to determine, in retrospect, whether Roosevelt's intransigence stemmed from his desire to aid England's plight, his determination to halt Japanese aggression, or a combination of the two. F.D.R. was the target of war pressures from several distinct directions. Chiang Kai-Shek constantly urged United States intervention, for China, at war with Japan, desperately needed American aid. Roosevelt's administrative assistant, a friend and admirer of the Soviets, also supported a United States stand against Japan. All this time Japan worked for peace negotiations with the United States, but her offers were continuously rejected. The United States was willing to accept no less than total Japanese capitulation to her demands.

On November 26th, two weeks before Pearl Harbor, Roosevelt sent the Japanese a ten-point ultimatum which he knew they could not accept and which he knew, as well, would eventuate in war. The Pacific war which did, indeed, result produced no more successful solutions than had the one in Europe. China was overrun by the Communists, who had only to overthrow a government weary and depleted from the long war, and the people of China, so long subjected to the privations of war, were receptive to the improvements Communism promised. The conversion of the world's largest population to Communism hardly qualified World War II as a success for the U.S. Further, Roosevelt's concession to Russia, at the expense of China, of a favored position in Manchuria similar to that from which Japan had been ousted by military force, was a contradiction of the very ideals for which America claimed to have entered the war. If self-determination had been America's primary goal in the Pacific, then the war was a failure. Why did the United States give Russia what Americans had fought so long to free from Japan? Why did she not consult China before making this concession? And, if Russia demanded this territory before it would consent to help defeat Japan, then what real purpose did the war serve?

Though the attack on Pearl Harbor came as a great shock to the American people, F.D.R. was surprised only by its target. He knew his demands had made war inevitable, and he had substantive evidence that war was about to begin. United States Navy radio receiving-stations intercepted a message on December 4, 1941 that was easily recognizable as a signal to Japanese representatives in Washington that attack was imminent. The meaning of the message was obvious to Navy radio-men because the United States had cracked Japan's diplomatic code and knew that a specific false weather report would signify impending attack. Pacific commanders had been warned previously to prepare for possible attack, but they were not alerted when the war message was broadcast. Nor did Roosevelt call an emergency conference of military leaders to devise defenses against anticipated strike. Why he failed to do so long has puzzled historians and military men. Furthermore, high-ranking officials in Washington realized Japan-based radio messages to their ambassador on December 7th probably indicated attack would occur that day, yet no warning was dispatched to United States military commanders at Pearl Harbor.

Some have accused Roosevelt of inciting the Japanese to attack American forces, letting them strike the first blow to arouse the American people sufficiently to enter the war in support of England and Churchill. More extreme is the charge that Roosevelt spurred America into war to achieve full production, optimum employment, and economic prosperity, thereby guaranteeing his popularity in office. It is unfortunate that Roosevelt was often publicly close-mouthed regarding national defense strategies because it made him suspect to many. Ironically, he stated in 1940:

> I have said it again and again and again. Your boys are not going to be sent into any foreign wars. They are going into training to form a force so strong that, by its very existence, it will keep the threat of war far away from our shores.

Isolationism prevailed among the American people at the time, and Roosevelt was campaigning for re-election. Yet, he knew war was almost inevitable. If he had really intended to avoid war, he would not have adopted a hard-line attitude with the Japanese but would earnestly have sought to negotiate a peaceful settlement.

Had American military commanders been alerted to the extreme imminence of attack, her Pearl Harbor fleet could have been prepared and total disaster averted. Certainly Sunday was the most suspect day of the week, since it enabled a surprise attack, with a large percentage of fleet personnel on liberty. The bulk of the Pacific fleet was headquartered in Pearl Harbor and was thus the logical attack target. Prior naval maneuvers had shown an attack on Pearl Harbor to be quite feasible. Yet Kimmel and Short, America's military leaders in Hawaii, received no warning from Washington of Japan's December 7th radio messages. While some historians term this a tragic oversight, others have made a case for the conscious withholding of information from military authorities at Honolulu. The attack on Pearl Harbor proved to be a great tactical success for the Japanese, who struck a hard first blow. But ultimately it was to mean their devastating defeat.

During the war years there was little "hysteria" in the United States except that against those of Japanese-American descent. German- and Italian-Americans went virtually unnoticed as Americans acknowledged they gave their first allegiance to the United States. Though Japanese-Americans also proved their good citizenship through participation in the war effort by outstanding service in America's armed forces, racism ran high against the Japanese, especially on the West Coast, where the majority of the nation's Nisei resided. Some 125,000 Japanese were resident in the continental United States, and most had been born in America. But the cry sounded,

> A Jap's a Jap. It makes no difference whether he's an American or not.

At first, anti-Nisei sentiments occurred on the individual level. Soon the funds of Japanese-Americans on deposit in California banks were frozen, and the depositors were refused check-cashing service. Before long milkmen refused to deliver their milk, insurance companies cancelled their policies, and grocers refused to sell them food. All this, although they were loyal American citizens. One Western newspaper carried a column ending,

> Let 'em be pinched, hurt, hungry, and dead up against it. . . . Personally I hate the Japanese.

Roosevelt finally signed an order to transport 110,000 Japanese in the West to detention camps and it was executed swiftly. The Japanese workers and families were thereby deprived of millions in yearly income and forced to relinquish their businesses, farms and equipment, and, in some cases, their life savings. No efforts were made to detect subversion. The Japanese were collected and imprisoned by the thousands, on only forty-eight hours' notice. This was all the time allotted them to dispose of their homes, businesses, and belongings! The United States Army supervised the mass evacuation, with the Japanese allowed to carry only hand-luggage into the camps. Once interned they were confined like criminals within barbed-wire confines, and under constant military patrol. These camps were all in desolate areas of the United States, and living conditions were very poor. Later in the war young American-born or naturalized Japanese were allowed to serve in the armed services, but only after careful screening. Even then, they were confined to segregated units. Their parents and families continued to be imprisoned in the internment camps.

During the early years of the war, the Japanese-American units were assigned only to the European front. Later, they served with extreme distinction in the Pacific Theater as well. At times they were so close to enemy lines that they could translate the enemy's overheard dialogue. One courageous Japanese-American youth, clad in a Japanese colonel's uniform, marched briskly into the enemy ranks and began to issue orders. He marched the entire unit right into the clutches of his waiting fellow soldiers, and all were taken prisoner. The ironic fact is that, throughout the wartime ordeal, the interned Japanese-Americans remained largely unembittered and loyal to the United States, despite their cruel confinement. Perhaps the most tragic aspect of their plight was the hopelessness of the older Nisei when they were freed at last. They did not know where to go nor what to do. Their security was shattered, and, fearful and confused, they could not easily readapt to American life. Many lived out their waning years lost and spiritually defeated.

It has long been a credo in wartime that military forces kill only the enemy and not civilians. This prompted the United States to criticize severely Japan's bombing of civilian centers early in World War II. These attacks were particularly abhorrent since they killed infants, women, children, and the elderly, as well as adult males. The Japanese air war was aimed at military and industrial centers, but often it also struck civilian residential sectors. Prior to entering the war, the United States had sharply rebuked Japan for these indiscriminate bombings of Asian cities. Thus, England, once she had declared war on Germany, hesitated to bomb German cities, fearful the wanton killing of civilians would alienate America. But within less than four years America's morality seemed to lapse, and she defeated Japan by inflicting the most devastating bombing in history, killing and mutilating countless thousands of civilians. The dropping of the atom-bomb on Hiroshima, and then Nagasaki to hasten the end of the war, revealed to the world that even this great democratic nation could not sustain its high ideals through the bloody slaughter of World War II. Prior to this the allies had issued a statement named the Potsdam Ultimatum, calling for Japan's surrender. It contained no reference to the horrendous weapon, as it should have were its real aim to achieve immediate surrender without undue bloodshed.

Over 100,000 persons were killed or maimed in Hiroshima alone. In the aftermath of radioactive fallout, thousands of children later proved to be diseased or deformed. The atom bomb dropped on Nagasaki scorched still another city from the face of the earth. America's use of the A-bomb in total secrecy and without warning was comparable in infamy to Japan's siege of Pearl Harbor, with the difference that in Hiroshima and Nagasaki countless thousands of civilians were also killed.

Later it was revealed that the United States government had conducted a secret poll of some 150 scientists who had developed the A-bomb. Most voted for a demonstration in some remote region of the bomb's terrifying power, thus, giving the Japanese forewarning of their grim fate if they did not surrender. The bomb so ruthlessly dropped on Hiroshima and Nagasaki has produced a threat greater than mankind has ever faced, one of total annihilation. Such was the harvest of World War II.

As World War II drew to a close in Europe the great allied powers met to decide the fate of the post-war world. Russia, which had lost 7,500,000 men in its struggle to defeat Hitler (compared to 292,000 for the United States and 555,000 for Britain) and, at one point, had fought nine-tenths of the German army, believed she had been chiefly instrumental in defeating the Axis. The Soviets thus demanded major concessions for their role in achieving the Allied victory which amounted to making many Eastern European countries subservient to the U.S.S.R. These demands were granted by Churchill and Roosevelt. Russia thus received the eastern sector of Poland, the result of her pact with Hitler according her part of the spoils from his Poland invasion. Yugoslavia was given over to a dictatorship under Tito. Latvia, Lithuania, and Estonia, plus specified lands on the Finnish border, were permanently annexed to Russia. The principle of self-determination for which the war had been fought was essentially scrapped. Russia's annexation of Eastern Poland and part of East Prussia, like the seizure of German territory for Poland, were clearly against the will of the peoples of these regions. These concessions produced millions of embittered, homeless refugees and created new borders destined to cause future conflicts.

The free democratic elections promised by the Russians to the people of Eastern Europe proved to be a mockery, as Roosevelt should have foreseen in the light of Red occupation practices in that area and the total absence of election controls and safeguards. Though Poland's resistance to Hitler had been the occasion of the war, that country was sacrificed at Yalta to the Soviets, much as Czechoslovakia had been sacrificed to Hitler at the Munich Conference in 1938. It was agreed that the Soviet dominated government exiled from Poland would serve as the nucleus of a provisional government until the promised "free elections" could be conducted.

Other surrenders of America's principles were also made at Yalta. Since German labor could be used as a source of reparations, slavery thereby was sanctioned for a large number of German war prisoners, who could be held in servitude for years after the war. German prisoners were held in England and France, but they gratefully avoided such a fate in Russia. A "fugitive slave law" was enacted when Roosevelt and Churchill agreed to return all Russian citizens resident in Western zones to Russia, even those refugees who did not wish to return. At Yalta the Western powers also gave Stalin control of Manchuria, the most industrialized sector of China, this without consulting or even informing the Chinese government, their ally. Along with this economic control over Manchuria the Russians also were given South Sakhalin and the Kurile Islands. The Russians held a large part of Eastern Europe. However, such control need not have meant the allies' automatic endorsement of their schemes for satellite regimes in those territories. Though the war had been fought to prevent just such domination, the Western powers' endorsement of these regimes all but guaranteed their existence and growth.

As the war neared its end high hopes prevailed in Eastern

Europe for freedom from Nazi tyranny. In the aftermath, however, the world saw that these hopes were futile: the Hungarian Revolution and Czechoslovakian uprising showed only too clearly how the Western powers turned over these countries from one totalitarian dominator to another. Russia, which had placed the Polish army under Russian military leaders, ousted all non-Communists from the governments of Hungary and Czechoslovakia, including the president of Czechoslovakia. The Soviet takeover proved that, once the Russians gained a political foothold, they would turn neighboring nations into puppet states.

One positive outcome of Churchill's and Roosevelt's conferences with Stalin was the agreement to draft a Charter for the proposed United Nations. While the union of nations that emerged has performed disappointingly as a peacemaker, it has made major contributions to the peoples of the world in other areas of human welfare, such as the educational and technical assistance programs of UNESCO. But even more important is its potential to grow someday into a mediator and peace-keeper for the world.

CHAPTER XII

Post-War Years: Bureaucracy and Blunder

When China's eight-year war with Japan came to a halt in 1945 with the end of World War II, Chiang Kai-Shek's Nationalist regime already was losing power. The United States continued to supply Chiang with arms to fight the Communist forces within China's borders. But the Chiang government had lost the confidence of the Chinese people, and even more devastating to its retention of power, it had lost the respect of its own troops.

Many of the arms supplied Chiang by the U.S. were pilfered and sold by corrupt officials within his regime, while others were abjectly surrendered to the Communists. Though Russia was supplying the Chinese Communists with weapons seized from the withdrawing Japanese, America provided Chiang's government with far greater amounts of arms and supplies. But this aid had no significant impact on the progress of either side. The Kuomintang government was failing; corruption within its ranks and failure to help the great masses of the impoverished Chinese people were the chief reasons contributing to its demise. Only the support of millions of American troops was maintaining it in power. Under Chiang the Kuomintang government had manifested little interest in instituting needed reforms and had taken almost no initiative to mobilize China's vast resources toward the creation of a great, self-sustaining nation. American leaders repeatedly urged Chiang to concentrate on sorely needed internal reforms rather than on measures to suppress his foes. But these urgings went unheeded.

President Harry S. Truman then dispatched General Marshall to attempt to persuade Chiang's Nationalist regime to form a coalition government with the Communists. The mission was in vain. When Washington at last cut back its arms appropriations for Nationalist China, the Chiang regime collapsed, a victim of its own inaction and corruption. However tragic the loss of this huge country to the Communists, the U.S. did not wish to sustain a government which had neither popular support nor the strength to stand on its own.

Following the Communist take-over in China two more wars erupted in the Orient: the Korean conflict and the civil war in Vietnam. Both centered about Communism, and in both, the United States became directly involved. Ironically, the Korean War, perhaps the most justified war in which the U.S. had ever been involved, was closely followed by one of its least justified military interventions, that in the mounting civil war raging between divided North and South Vietnam.

The Korean War, a concerted effort by world nations and the Korean people to halt an onslaught of Communist aggression, had great international significance because the effort to help South Korea was led not by the United States or any other individual country, but by the United Nations. The Korean conflict thus represented discernable recognition of the potential and power of the concept of world government, as well as a cooperative action by members of a world body acting in concert to halt totalitarian aggression. Thus, in effect, the strategic issue of the Korean War was secondary; whether the Communists held South Korea or not made little difference in the world's military balance of power. Korea was an economically backward nation which required vast sums of foreign aid. Her seizure and subsidy by the Communists might have been viewed by some world powers as a welcome solution to a long-term problem. Yet the successful resolution of the military conflict which began in Korea in 1950 presents a measure of hope to all nations that, one day, a strong, cohesive world government will achieve sufficient support and stature to successfully police the actions and aggressions of all nations.

The significance of the Korean conflict may also be seen in

the factors leading up to the attempted Communist takeover. After World War II Soviet forces held Korea north of the 38th parallel. The U.S.S.R. thereafter organized a Communist regime in that area. In an effort to avert the Communist build-up the United Nations in 1947 passed a resolution calling for nationwide fall elections in Korea. The Soviets defied the U.N. order and two separate Korean states thereby came into existence.

On June 25, 1950, the Communist North Koreans launched a sudden surprise attack on South Korea, perhaps influenced by the recent revelation of U.S. Secretary of State Dean Acheson that the Republic of Korea lay beyond the U.S. defense perimeter. Acheson's ill-advised statement indicated that the United States probably would not defend South Korea in the event she were invaded by North Korean forces. Only Japan and the Philippines were to be defended, according to the U.S. plan, Korea being excluded chiefly because it was strategically unimportant. But when the attack on South Korea came, the nations which had so recently defeated Hitler realized Korea was precisely the model of the small weak nation which the United Nations had been created to protect. The United States thus took the lead in the United Nations Security Council, presenting a proposal to declare North Korea an aggressor and to supply military aid to South Korea. Once the proposal was approved, many United Nation member nations contributed military units to power the police action in Korea, with the United States contributing the greatest number of troops since it then had the largest body of non-Communist military manpower in the Pacific area. At least fifteen United Nations member countries contributed fighting troops to the South Korean cause, while five more sent non-combatant medical units. America's Pacific Commander, General Douglas MacArthur, was designated Supreme Commander of the United Nations forces.

MacArthur led the United Nations' forces northward through embattled South Korea, driving back the invaders. After MacArthur's forces had recaptured most of South and North Korea, hopes for a united Korea were dashed when Chinese Communists intervened in force to help the North Korean armies and drove United Nations forces back to the region of the 38th parallel. Thereafter, a stalemate was effected between both sides. The line where the United Nations' troops had dug in and successfully held their ground became the permanent boundary dividing North and South.

United States leaders hinted they might resort to the use of "tactical atomic weapons" to break the Korean stalemate. This announcement may have led Communist China to agree to a truce. But the premise again was made clear; even atomic weapons are not too horrible or devastating to use if the need —and goal—seem great enough.

The combined action of the United Nations to protect the sovereignty of South Korea demonstrated clearly that united world government need entail neither the appeasement of Communism nor passivity in the face of aggression. Though the military defense of South Korea was provided chiefly by the United States, no evidence exists that future police actions by a world body could not be more equally staffed by all participant nations. The united defense of South Korea was successful in every aspect except one: that of the failure of all efforts to reunite the divided North and South.

In 1951 the world witnessed a startling event; General Douglas MacArthur was fired by President Harry Truman. Whereas the U.S. government believed the containment of Communism and the prevention of a third world war to be paramount tasks, General MacArthur advocated what appeared to be all-out war on China, an action which posed potentially dire consequences. Such a war would have left Europe and the Middle East virtually undefended by the U.S. and would thereby have enabled Russia to penetrate these areas more deeply. The U.S.S.R. may have entered the proposed war on the side of China, thereby bringing on World War III. MacArthur was informed by Truman that he was to continue fighting a limited war and was not to invade China. MacArthur's plan to declare war on China having been rejected by the Administration, he began to express his displeasure to the press. In one interview after another MacArthur recited his proposals and criticized the Administration for rejecting them. Truman ordered the Joint Chiefs of Staff to remind the general that all policy statements were to be cleared through the Pentagon, but MacArthur continued to air his views in what hinted to be calculated insubordination. Truman thus had no choice but to recall him. Whatever merits MacArthur's proposal may have had, he had transgressed upon one tenet essential to the success of a democracy: civil authority must hold ultimate control over the nation's military.

Following his recall General MacArthur was welcomed on his return to the United States by teeming throngs in every major city and accorded a hero's reception. His famed speech to a joint session of Congress prompted one congressman to say, "We heard God speak here today, God in the flesh, the voice of God." So great was the tide of public sentiment for MacArthur that the Senate Foreign Relations and Armed Services Committees united to conduct a full-scale hearing on the General's ouster, but the results were almost wholly partisan, with the Democratic members endorsing Truman's action and the Republicans siding with MacArthur. The Democrats were in the majority. This partisanship was unfortunate because, in a working democracy, the right and duty of the President to govern all military officials must be absolute and unquestionable.

As U.S. troops fought Communist aggression in Korea, Senator Joseph McCarthy launched an attack against so-called "subversives" within America. He charged that all levels of American government were infiltrated with Communists and he led a spirited personal crusade to purge the "Reds." McCarthy's questionable goal was largely motivated by his desire for personal fame and power. Perhaps the most unfortunate result of his "witch-hunts" was that they gained such widespread public notice and support. Often without even supportive evidence, the Senator defamed the reputations of innocent Americans, branding them "Reds" and "Pinkos," charges which he hurled increasingly in every direction. He linked public officials, educators, actors, persons of prominence at all levels with the alleged "Communist conspiracy." A Senate Committee headed by Millard Tydings exposed the baselessness of many of McCarthy's charges, but the mendacious McCarthy continued to level his accusations and countless thousands of Americans believed them valid. McCarthy traveled to Maryland to work to defeat Senator Tydings, and in a tactic he had used against other Congressmen who dared oppose him he publicly declared that Communism even "extended its tentacles into the United States Senate."

Many in government feared the power of McCarthy, and this growing fear gave the Senator power. During his several-year reign as the foremost American demagogue, McCarthy accused almost every prominent politician of tending toward "softness" on Communism. He devastated reputation after reputation as Americans everywhere questioned whether there wasn't some basis of truth in his charges. For instance, General Marshall, a leader whose sterling character and valuable contributions to America were widely known, was challenged and defamed by McCarthy, who claimed he was part of a "conspiracy so immense and an infamy so black as to dwarf any previous venture in the history of man."

In 1954 McCarthy announced his plans for a broad investigation of U.S. Army leaders, whom he accused of "blackmailing" his investigating committee. The Army-McCarthy hearings thereafter were televised throughout the U.S., and in their course, exposed the ruthless ill will of the Senator. His public popularity declined, and only then did his fellow Senators dare stand up to him, voting at last for his censure. Countless Americans had indeed been swayed by the power tactics of a living demagogue, and many who later saw "McCarthyism" bared as a ruthless, reckless bid for political power were ashamed of their gullibility. Still others, long after McCarthy's demise, continued to hunt "Communists" behind every political, educational and cultural door for years to come.

The United States after the Korean War was repeatedly frustrated in its efforts to implement a successful foreign policy. The Eisenhower administration tried to regain ground after the many post-World War II concessions granted the Communists. Eisenhower's Secretary of State, John Foster Dulles, announced in a radio broadcast to Eastern Europe in 1953, "You can count on us," thereby raising the hopes of thousands of Europeans who had lost their freedom after World War II. Thereafter, in June, 1953, East German workers rioted, and in 1956, a large-scale revolution erupted in Hungary. But in neither instance did the United States venture the help Dulles had promised. Though the United States could not risk world war to assist these revolutions, it was unfortunate that its earlier promises of aid had raised the hopes of oppressed peoples and contributed to their uprisings. One Hungarian refugee made clear this disappointment after the revolution in his homeland had been smashed: "We can never believe the West again." Such betrayals of promised support diminished America's stature worldwide, a decline intensified by still further U.S. blunders in its diplomatic foreign relations.

In one such failure, anti-American sentiments in Latin America soared in 1954 following the overthrow of the Guatemalan government. It was widely known that the overthrow had been organized by the United States' Central Intelligence Agency. Guatemala at the time was ruled by a pro-Red administration and American leaders registered alarm when she began to import Russian-made arms from behind the Iron Curtain. America's alarm and disdain for pro-Communist governments near her boundaries intensified with the anxiety that revolutionary rule might spread to other Latin American countries. This growing concern unfortunately motivated the U.S. to act in ways that ignored and overrode the right of the Guatemalan people to self-determination.

America thus supplied arms to an ex-Guatemalan army officer in Honduras, who, with his anti-government forces, was thereby enabled to march into Guatemala and overthrow its government. Guatemala's ousted President Arbenz called on the United Nations Security Council to investigate the revolutionary overthrow, terming it essentially an uprising spurred by the United States, and thus, hostile aggression by a foreign power. United States representatives to the world council vetoed the bid for United Nations action, thereby disclosing America's guilt. Had the United States been innocent of Arbenz's charges it could only have been vindicated by such an investigation.

Many claim that in its Guatemalan intervention America acted not to stop Communism but to protect the major interests of the American Fruit Company in Guatemala. In a 1965 press conference ex-President Eisenhower openly admitted the United States had planned the Guatemalan overthrow and had supported it with gifts of weapons and planes to the revolutionaries. Whatever the motivations that caused this reprehensible aggression, America's prestige in Latin America suffered in its wake. The anti-Yankee sentiments engendered thereby were clear during Vice-President Nixon's tour of South America in 1958. He was mobbed, stoned, pelted with eggs, and finally forced to abandon his tour.

America's credibility and prestige among world nations were damaged even further during the Eisenhower administration by the U-2 incident. In 1960, on a surveillance flight deep within the Soviet Union, a high-flying American plane was sighted and shot down by the Russians. The trespasses of American military planes flying over the USSR were considered acts of aggression by Russia, and Soviet leaders cleverly used the U-2 incident to denounce America to the world. How would America react, Khrushchev asked, if Soviet military planes flew missions over the United States? Would not the United States consider such flights extremely provocative, if not openly aggressive?

The United States further undermined its stature during the course of the U-2 incident by lying about the nature of the flight. Assuming the U-2 pilot to have been killed in the downing of the plane, a State Department spokesman announced that the aircraft was a "weather plane" which accidentally had strayed across the Turkish border into Soviet skies. The U-2 pilot, Francis G. Powers, was alive however, and admitted to his Russian captors that his flight had been one of numerous flights conducted by the United States over Russia for the purpose of photographing key military installations. Powers thereby revealed the flight was no "accident," as the U.S. State Department had claimed. Armed with this statement the USSR exposed America's lie to the world, adding that the photographs recovered from the U-2 wreckage were not of weather formations but of military installations situated more than 1,000 miles within Soviet borders.

President Eisenhower announced "personal responsibility" for the flight, thereby declaring it an official act of the United States rather than one authorized by some lesser official. Though Eisenhower soon announced the cessation of further U-2 flights, he refused to apologize for the prior trespasses into Soviet skies, thus compounding America's breach of responsibility in the eyes of many world nations. The incident, passed off by military and White House spokesmen to the American people as a pecadillo, appeared along with America's subsequent falsehoods to comprise an act of bad faith to most of the world. In Japan, for example, anti-American feelings ran so high as a result of the incident that the Japanese government cancelled Eisenhower's upcoming tour.

Soon after the U-2 incident, America's invasion of the Bay of Pigs occurred in 1961, sorely injuring relations between the U.S. and Latin America. The invasion grew out of the overthrow in 1959 by Dr. Fidel Castro of Cuba's corrupt dictatorship. He established a Communist regime in the island nation. Alarmed at the rise of a Communist nation close to her shores, the United States mapped secret plans to overthrow Castro. The Central Intelligence Agency, so closely linked to the successful overthrow of Guatemala's government a few years earlier, implemented the U.S. plan by training several thousand exiled Cubans in Central America, arming and transporting them to Cuban shores. But the Cuban people remained loyal to Castro's government, contrary to the Central Intelligence Agency's predictions, and the invasion of the Bay of Pigs proved a total failure. Once again, as in the Guatemalan overthrow, it demonstrated that America willfully ignored the right of other peoples to choose their own government when these governments were not to the liking of the U.S. The failure of the Bay of Pigs invasion prompted the U.S.S.R. to assume a more aggressive role in the Cold War, while also giving her an excuse to establish and fortify missile-bases in Cuba for the purpose of "defending" the island.

In 1962, an event occurred which, in its implications regarding the future of man, overshadowed other events of the '60's—the Cuban missile crisis. For this event revealed facts which, taken together, show a nuclear holocaust between the world's great powers is possible. The Cuban missile crisis, like Hiroshima before it, left a black cloud of fear hanging over the world, with the seeming eventuality of a nuclear holocaust that could end all life on earth.

After the Bay of Pigs fiasco, Russia provided Cuba with defensive missiles, planes and a retinue of military advisors. The attempted invasion revealed what Russian officials had genuinely feared: that the United States might attack Cuba and seek to establish a government there under its control. Thus, in 1962, the Russians began to build missile silos in Cuba for launching intermediate-range offensive missiles capable of delivering nuclear warheads up to one-thousand miles. United States surveillance aircraft violating Cuban air space just as it had over Russia, photographed the building of these installations. Immediately, a crisis was precipitated. President Kennedy expressed determination to bar all "offensive weapons" from Cuba, but the differentiation between offensive and defensive weapons was questionable where nuclear armaments were concerned. The greater part of America's defense then, as now, consisted of offensive missiles designed for use as "deterrents." The threat of massive retaliation was considered America's primary defense. In this same sense, the Cuban missiles could legitimately be termed defensive weapons.

Rightly or wrongly, President Kennedy regarded the placement of missiles in Cuba as an act of war, and acted throughout the crisis as though Russia were attacking the United States. He ordered a U.S. Navy blockade of a large sea perimeter 500 miles from Cuba, then announced to Russia that no missiles would be allowed to pass through the blockade and that all incoming Soviet ships would be searched. A naval blockade traditionally is akin to an act of war.

What of the Cubans' rights to self-determination? Did she not have the right to erect missile sites with Russia's help just as other world powers have done with America's help? At the time Jupiter missiles had been stationed for five years right on Russia's frontier, in Turkey, a NATO ally of the United States. These missiles also were "offensive" in nature and were capable of striking points far within the Soviet Union. In regard to these missiles in Turkey. Khrushchev wrote Kennedy during the Cuban crisis:

> You are worried over Cuba. You say that it worries you because it lies at a distance of 90 miles across the sea from the shores of the United States. However, Turkey lies next to us. Our sentinels are pacing up and down and watching each other. Do you believe you have the right to demand security for your country, and the removal of such weapons that you qualify as offensive, while not recognizing the right for us?

> You have stationed devastating rocket weapons, which you call offensive, in Turkey, literally right next to us. How then does recognition of our equal military possibilities tally with such unequal relations between our great states. . . .

Khrushchev's message was clear: how could the United States maintain missiles along the Soviet borders, yet term a similar act by Russia near her shores an "attack" on the United States? Khrushchev's point was well made. He went on to venture a compromise: Russia's removal of its missiles and sites in Cuba in exchange for America's removal of its missiles and sites in Turkey. President Kennedy refused to negotiate the proposed compromise, insisting that only the Cuban missiles were important and that they must be removed immediately. In truth, the proposed compromise would have cost the United States prestige in Turkey, but would have had no military significance. Kennedy, in fact, had ordered removal of the Jupiter missiles from Turkey two months earlier, since by then, they were obsolete. But when the Russians asked for this concession he flatly refused. Kennedy was concerned that America be taken seriously—that the Communists learn that they could not bully the United States. Through firmness the President hoped to avoid an escalating conflict.

199

During the spiralling tension U.S. nuclear missiles were readied for firing and their crews placed on maximum alert, ready to launch an attack. Personnel assigned to I.B.M. sites in the Western U.S., capable of delivering a massive attack on the U.S.S.R., were placed on a 70-hour work week. America's B-52 bombers were mobilized and kept in the air at all times by the Strategic Air Command, ready to launch an atomic attack instantly on orders. Each carried a full load of nuclear bombs. Orders quickly concentrated U.S. ground and air forces in Florida, ready to attack Cuba if Russia did not withdraw her missiles.

Throughout those tense days of 1962, even a minor incident could have detonated the deadly atomic charge on either side. An American U-2 plane strayed from its course over Alaska into the Russian Chukotskiy Peninsula, a perilous incident at a time when such a bomber might be thought to carry nuclear weapons. Fortunately the Soviets took no punitive action, and the plane and pilot returned unscathed to American territory. But Khrushchev wrote Kennedy in indignation, "What is this, a provocation? One of your planes violates our frontier during this anxious time we are both experiencing, when everything has been put into combat readiness. Is it not a fact that an intruding American plane could easily be taken for a nuclear bomber, which might push us to a fateful step?"

Thereafter United States U-2 spy planes continued to fly over Cuba, while American ships formed a war-time blockade around Cuba. Had shooting begun accidentally or had a Russian ship inadvertently been sunk, Russia's military strategists probably would not have been able to withdraw their armada as they did, and full-scale war could have ensued. Khrushchev, the man who earlier had pounded his shoe on the table at the United Nations, must have found it difficult to back down, yet fortunately he did so. Thus, Kennedy beamed the following message to Moscow via the Voice of America:

> I welcome Chairman Khrushchev's statesmanlike decision to stop building bases in Cuba, dismantling offensive weapons and returning them to the Soviet Union under United

Nations verification. This is an important and constructive contribution to peace.

This was probably Khrushchev's finest hour, for though he and his country had suffered a loss of prestige, his decision may have saved the world.

As the crisis ended, the world breathed a sigh of relief. Kennedy's firmness, although terribly dangerous, was successful. Russian offensive missiles were not brought into Cuba and nuclear war was avoided. The crisis bared an important reality for America—that the President was empowered to make war even without Congressional declaration. Coupled with modern weaponry, this meant the President could commit the United States to a war that would be over before Congress even had time to convene. Twentieth Century technology thus altered one major tenet of the American Constitution. A vital check between the three major branches of American government had been lost. Now, even without Congressional approval, the President can plunge the United States into world war.

Since the Bay of Pigs invasion and its stormy aftermath, United States efforts to improve relations with the Latin American nations through monetary aid and technical assistance have made slow progress. Fear of U.S. domination stemming from America's interference in the governments of neighboring nations looms large among the Latin peoples. The economic rewards promised by Communist powers appeal to many.

One recent instance of U.S. interference in the internal affairs of a Latin American nation by means of military force occurred in 1965 in the Dominican Republic. The American intervention stemmed from a rebellion which had broken out earlier against the military dictatorship that ruled the tiny nation. United States leaders feared that Communist forces might be dominant in the rebel group. Thus, one week after the revolt, President Lyndon B. Johnson dispatched U.S. Marines into the Dominican Republic on the pretense of protecting Americans and other aliens present there. While no other foreign power intervened or ventured aid to the rebel forces, United States strategists nonetheless prepared to subdue them on the allegation that their leaders were of Communist persuasion. Numerous Latin American leaders criticized America for her invasion. Even some good friends of the United States objected that Communist motivation in the rebellion was minimal. In her repeated meddling and domination of the affairs of other nations the United States ironically resembled the U.S.S.R., which similarly dominates those in its "sphere of influence." Yet critics of America's foreign policy observe that the U.S., in charting a similar unprincipled course of self-interest as the Russians, has done so with greater bumbling and fewer successes. The Guatemalan overthrow, the Bay of Pigs fiasco and the invasion of the Dominican Republic all lend credence to this claim.

CHAPTER XIII

The Tragedy of Vietnam

Still, America's diplomatic blunders of the 1950's and early 1960's are trifling compared to her involvement in Vietnam. The involvement is understandable: since World War II, the United States had concentrated on containing the spread of Communism. This dedication, however, was to draw the U.S. into a tragic error in Vietnam as it entered perhaps the least justified war in its history. Even many who believed in concerted action against aggression condemned America's involvement in Vietnam on the basis that the Vietnamese War was not waged to repel aggression. Similarly, widespread protests echoed throughout the United States for nearly a decade as millions of Americans decried their nation's costly and ill-advised interference in the Southeast Asian conflict.

The beginnings of this conflict can be traced to as early as 1945, when the defeated Japanese, in the course of their surrender, withdrew their occupation forces from Vietnam. Before French forces could resume their control of the country, Vietminh partisans under Ho Chi Minh formed the "Democratic Republic of Vietnam" under the banner of independence. "Vietminh" was the name designating the alliance of Vietnamese nationalist organizations, a coalition of groups that believed Vietnam should be self-governing. Vietnam, at the time, was rife with disorder and crime, lacking any semblance of leadership. In the turmoil the Vietminh established a provisional government, proclaiming Vietnam an independent republic. The French nonetheless carried out their reoccupation. After a brief but unsuccessful period of negotiations over Vietnamese autonomy, war erupted between the French and the Vietnamese.

From 1946 until 1954 the Vietnamese fought valiantly for their independence, at a cost of one-million lives. The alliance of Vietnamese political groups was led by Ho Chi Minh, the father of the Vietnamese nation. The Vietminh waged vigorous guerilla warfare, and French planes and tanks failed to subdue them. The Vietminh claimed strong popular support, and the Vietnamese forces had the psychological advantage of fighting for independence on their home ground. At that time numerous American officials including Secretary of State Dulles denounced the Vietminh as "aggressors," a curious accusation against those who were defending their own soil in a struggle for independence. The French made offers of what they termed "independence," but these in fact, only guaranteed the continuance of French interests. France also proposed to convert Vietnam into a monarchy, headed by a French puppet leader, but the Vietnamese rejected this false gesture of freedom.

During those eight years of embittered conflict the United States supplied over two-billion dollars to the French campaign against the Vietnamese, covering a major share of the costs. The United States thereby hoped to help avert a Vietnamese revolution like that which had occurred in China, giving rise to a new Communist government. For the U.S., however, it proved a costly and tragic error to carry its containment policy to the extent of intervening in a people's quest to gain independence. Despite American aid the French forces suffered a major defeat at Dien Bien Phu in 1954. It was then that several other leading world powers, fearful of being drawn into the conflict that conceivably could trigger the beginning of World War III, joined to effect an armistice in Vietnam.

The resulting agreement, signed at Geneva in 1954, dictated a fair and seemingly sensible plan. Vietnam was to be divided into two zones, but the agreement emphasized these zones were merely temporary and that the 17th Parallel would in no way serve as a political boundary. The French were to occupy the Southern zone, the Vietnamese nationals the Northern one. Fighting was thereby ended, and the French were enabled to put their affairs in order before withdrawing from their Indo-China colony.

The Geneva Agreement made provisions for divided Vietnam to be quickly reunited. Within two years, the Geneva pact declared, a national election, to be supervised by an international commission headed by a representative from India, would enable the Vietnamese people to choose the government they desired. In the interim the Geneva Agreement permitted the Vietnamese to relocate from one zone to another if they so desired. Thousands in each sector took advantage of this opportunity. Ho Chi Minh abided by the terms of the Geneva Agreement, confident that the voice of the people would be heard at last in the upcoming election. President Eisenhower, in his book *Mandate for Change,* acknowledged that Ho would have been elected president of Vietnam had the promised election been held: ". . . had elections been held . . . possibly 80% of the population would have voted for the Communist Ho Chi Minh as their leader rather than (pro-Western Emperor) Bao Dai."

The interim government of the Southern zone, which assumed power when the defeated French withdrew, was composed largely of self-seekers struggling for positions of power, but who were doing little toward enacting needed reforms. The United States dispatched aid to the South in return for the interim government's promise that the reforms would be made.

Then, in 1956, Vietnam's former emperor, Bao Dai, was deposed. A Vietnamese aristocrat, Ngo Dinh Diem, then living in New York, was installed by the United States as President of South Vietnam. The appointment came as no surprise to many in Washington, D. C. Eisenhower, Nixon and Dulles liked Diem, and his popularity with these American leaders was sufficient assurance of his power. That same year, the reunifying national election stipulated by the Geneva Agreement was to be held in Vietnam. But Diem refused to permit the election to be held in the South. The United States, whose money and arms kept Diem in power, made no move to force him to comply with this guarantee of the Geneva Agreement. Indeed, it may be that the U.S. convinced Diem to refuse to permit the prescribed election, knowing Communist candidates would triumph in free popular election. If so, the self-seeking Diem needed little convincing.

Since the Eisenhower administration continued the policy initiated by Franklin D. Roosevelt of withholding areas of diplomatic information from the American people, few Americans knew the U.S. had installed Diem at the helm of power and were supporting his government. Nor was this the only transgression of the U.S., which in 1956 supplied military aircraft to South Vietnam, thus violating another article of the Geneva Agreement, which stipulated that neither Vietnamese zone was to receive military aid or make alliances with any foreign power. Diem is said to have remarked at the time that "the borders of the United States extend to the 17th Parallel." Thereafter, until the late 1960's, the army of South Vietnam was maintained almost entirely by American aid. Even more surprising is that the expenses of the "South Vietnamese" government also were borne by the United States. America supported an illegal government in South Vietnam and flagrantly violated the Geneva Agreement in the effort to protect her political interests in Southeast Asia.

The United States-supported Diem regime proved to be cruel and corrupt. Diem removed the village chiefs who had been elected according to long-time tradition by the villagers, and replaced them with his appointed officials. He brought to an end freedom of speech and of the press in South Vietnam and instituted sham elections. The *New York Times* reported that, in one such election, Diem's brother allegedly received 99.9% of the vote, while his sister-in-law received 99.4%. Wholesale arrests of Vietnamese nationalists and other dissidents were common as Diem asserted his power. Some 30,000 nationalists filled South Vietnam prison camps to the brim. With a growing reign of terror Diem sought to silence all dissidents by means of raids, plunder, and torture. These terror tactics spurred the South Vietnamese, though lacking weaponry or outside aid, to rebel against Diem. Nationalists, Communists, village leaders, and Buddhists banded together in the effort to overthrow Diem in an alliance named the National Liberation Front. The aims of their program were to form a coalition government in South Vietnam, institute democratic freedom, pursue a neutral foreign policy, develop public education programs, and institute land reforms. Most of those aligned with the NLF were not invading a foreign country. In fact, a majority of the South Vietnam leaders had migrated from the North. The North Vietnamese felt no qualms about aiding their countrymen to the South, since both sectors comprised a single nation. They viewed Diem as a despot and foreign-supported agent, who, in his refusal to permit the Vietnamese free elections, barred the way to reunity for North and South Vietnam.

The United States supported the Diem regime with military aid averaging $1,000,000 a day in cost, plus 10,000 U.S. military "advisors" to organize and train Diem's army. Those who advised forcing Diem to make needed reforms which would have alleviated conditions that triggered the revolution were ignored. However, as Diem's terror tactics and unpopularity mounted, the United States began to air its displeasure with him. At the time Diem was attempting to work out a deal with Ho Chi Minh, but the possibility of a reunification with the Communist North was unacceptable to the U.S. Lastly, Diem's popularity in Washington fell because he was a strident Vietnamese nationalist who accepted U.S. help but would not allow Washington to dictate policy. Diem's growing disfavor with the U.S. served as a sign to Diem's generals that America soon would favor a coup. Diem was deposed and shot!

The two years that followed, 1963 to 1965, saw one regime after another, eight in all, rise to power in South Vietnam, and then decline. The United States grew alarmed that should the growing discontent foment rebellion North and South Vietnam would be reunited. Thus it stepped up its military assistance to the Saigon government. As this new U.S. aid program began, America was actually involving itself in a war, one which it was doomed to lose. U.S. officials sought to justify their approval of large-scale military aid to the Saigon government on the claim that the North Vietnamese were aiding the NLF. In truth only a few hundred North Vietnamese troops were in South Vietnam at the time. What actually induced the offer of U.S. aid was that the Saigon government was losing its war with the rebels, thereby placing American interests in Indochina in jeopardy. Thus, the U.S. approved military support for that corrupt government and dispatched hundreds of thousands of its troops to Vietnam. Candidate Lyndon B. Johnson declared in his 1964 election campaign, "We are not about to send American boys nine or ten thousand miles away from home to do what Asian boys ought to be doing for themselves." Once elected, Johnson sent a half-million American boys to Vietnam. But, despite continuous predictions from Washington that with American aid the war would soon be won, the United States had little chance of winning a foreign war being fought by a people desperately bent on wresting freedom from foreign intervention, and fought on a guerilla basis at that.

Their difficulty in gaining victories and the acknowledged futility they faced in trying to subjugate an entire people led the Saigon government and the U.S. military to adapt brutal measures, often disregarding human life. This was particularly evident in the soaring civilian death rate. It had always been difficult to distinguish civilians from military personnel in Vietnam. Vietnamese villagers might live and farm with their families, yet ardently support the Viet Cong. In prior wars the United States military traditionally had limited aggression to military targets, enemy soldiers, artillery, military aircraft, and war production centers. Except at Hiroshima and Nagasaki a concerted effort had been made to avoid killing civilians. In Vietnam, however, civilians, including women, children, and the elderly, were killed in large numbers. Bomber raids by U.S. forces killed and maimed hapless civilians. Countless villages were bombed and strafed on the suspicion that Viet Cong were hiding there. Military intelligence, however, often lagged several days behind, so that the target Viet Cong had moved on to other villages before the appointed raids. While the American public largely decried the wholesale murder of civilians committed by Lieutenant Calley and other American troops at My Lai, similar massacres were also perpetrated from the air by U.S. bomber crews. Congressman Zablocki, reporting to the House Foreign Affairs Committee after his 1966 trip to

Vietnam, reported that about twice as many Vietnamese civilians were being killed yearly in the war as Viet Cong.

America's massive air power was also used to decimate large Vietnam areas designated "free strike zones." It had been announced that anyone present in these zones after a given date would be considered a Viet Cong soldier or sympathizer, and thus a legitimate target. However, many an impoverished Vietnamese resident of the "zones" refused to abandon the land they had owned for years. Thus when the threatened attack came, many civilians, their livestock, and their houses were targets of the merciless bombings. Even their crops were ravaged by fire bombs, leaving those who managed to survive no means of subsistence.

The atrocities perpetrated by the United States air war in Vietnam did not end there. When the American infantry engaged the enemy, heavy air and artillery fire was often called into action and enemy positions barraged with bombs and shell. In small, densely populated Vietnam, it was almost inevitable that stray explosives would kill and maim countless thousands of civilians in the target areas.

American napalm raids also victimized Vietnamese civilians. Napalm was often dropped on Vietnam villages, forcing the people to flee into open areas, where succeeding planes dropped fragmentation bombs, killing or injuring everybody in sight. It has been estimated that six times as many civilians as Viet Cong were killed in such napalm raids. Also a plan was implemented that sought to starve the Viet Cong into submission by destroying crops in Viet Cong-occupied areas. The plan extracted its toll among hordes of civilian victims. While adult males survived such shortages well, children and infants suffered malnutrition and even starvation. Even the use of these barbarous tactics did not enable America to win the war, nor did they help America's stature at home or abroad. This "war of attrition" failed both militarily and diplomatically.

President Lyndon B. Johnson, pressured by constant criticism from Americans irate at the nation's involvement in Vietnam, declined to run for the Presidency in 1968. Richard M. Nixon thereafter won the election with the promise of withdrawing U.S. troops from Vietnam. Troop withdrawal was indeed enforced by Nixon, but at an agonizingly slow pace. As U.S. troop numbers slowly decreased, remaining American forces were launched into neighboring countries several times. Under President Nixon the bombing of North Vietnam was resumed and heavy Naval seiges ordered. When ground troops were finally withdrawn from Vietnam, many were moved to neighboring countries. In 1973 the U.S. continued military involvement in Indochina after the Vietnam peace treaty had been signed. President Nixon without the knowledge or consent of Congress sent U.S. bombers in raids over Cambodia. A pilot involved in this Cambodian bombing admitted to the press that hospitals were important targets of the raids.

America's involvement in South Vietnam did not foster a working democracy there. In Saigon's 1967 presidential elections, American-backed candidates Ky and Thieu decided who might run against them, vetoing any candidate who advocated South Vietnamese neutrality or favored negotiations to end the war. Since the names of members of the National Liberation Front were barred from the ballot, no true measure of the public popularity of the South Vietnamese government was possible. Ky stated repeatedly prior to the election that he would stage a coup were anyone elected who did not "meet the aspirations of the people." The *New York Times* (August, 1967) quoted the Premier as saying that, were a civilian elected, he nevertheless would have to follow the policies laid down by the *junta,* that is, the military dictatorship headed by Thieu. Thieu and Ky together received only 35% of the votes cast in this weighted election in which they had successfully excluded all real opponents. In 1971 the South Vietnamese elections were even more farcical than they had been four years earlier. President Thieu ran for the Presidency totally unopposed, having shut out all rivals. Despite this despotic feat, the United States continued to support his regime.

The limited support that existed for the Saigon government largely was purchased by the United States with bribes. Colonel David Hackworth, probably the most-decorated U.S. officer in Vietnam active duty at the time of his resignation in 1971, discussed a major reason underlying the Viet Cong's continuous military triumphs over Saigon. He stated the Viet Cong were highly motivated, determined fighters who believed in their cause, while the South Vietnamese were "motivated by a new Honda, a Rolex watch, a refrigerator or a fan, or how many goodies you can get from the PX . . ."

In 1971 a series of secret documents stolen from the Pentagon were published in the *New York Times* and other newspapers. These "Pentagon Papers" revealed plainly the miscalculations and blunders which had led America into the Vietnamese war. One U.S. administration after another had miscalculated the will of the Vietnamese people to resist, relying too heavily on "game plans" which served to dehumanize the enemy and made killing seemingly remote. Ironically, the U.S. intervention in Vietnam had driven that country toward a closer relationship with Communist China, traditionally an enemy of Vietnam. In addition, world opinion was generally unfavorable to America's presence in Vietnam. Strategically, for the U.S., the war was a failure.

The United States lost some 50,000 young men in the Vietnam war, and over 300,000 were wounded. Over two-hundred billion U.S. dollars were spent. All this in a disgraceful effort to keep a corrupt government in power against the wishes of its people.

The Future

The United States today is the most powerful nation in the history of civilization. Its citizens enjoy material wealth in unprecedented abundance. Yet such fundamental problems as urban overcrowding, pollution, discrimination against women and ethnic minorities, and the threat of nuclear war, plague the nation. A great challenge confronts America. Her material abundance, her massive wealth achieved, can she now eradicate the weighty problems of pollution, corruption, discrimination and overpopulation so that her material abundance will truly reflect a serene and privileged life?

At a time when solutions to many of these major problems are in sight, if only on the distant horizon, the grim specter of nuclear war still hangs menacingly over America. Yet the United States has also made the minor beginnings toward solving the greatest problem in the history of man—war. From the United States came the incipient beginnings of world government. President Wilson conceived the League of Nations, a concept which, at the end of World War II, gave form to the United Nations, in whose creation the United States played a major role. One day the American statehood system may provide the model for an effective world organization of nations, one in which specific powers, such as worldwide defense against aggression, would rest in the international institution, while other powers, such as education and economic planning, would remain with each individual nation. If such an organization judiciously and conscientiously controlled the world's stockpile of nuclear weapons, the grim possibility of nuclear annihilation would be dispelled and at the same time totalitarian aggression could be checked. Yet America would still be free to pursue her remarkable development in economics, medicine, science and technology. Her material wealth and abundance, her outstanding fund of human and capital resources would still be hers to use, and her cultural heritage of individual freedoms and democracy would remain inviolable. Unburdened by the threats of outside aggression and the lingering, costly involvement in foreign wars, she could concentrate her incredible resources on the conquest of environmental pollution, poverty and disease.

Another important question faces America: can the people of the United States retain their idealism and desire to eradicate their nation's problems? Events have conspired to demoralize, hopefully only temporarily, the American people. The tragic war in Vietnam led to disillusionment in every sector of America. Some were distraught to find that the United States could not win a war against a tiny Asian nation. For others there was disenchantment, even outrage, over the war's lack of justifiability. All were horrified to hear reports of the brutal techniques used at times to fight it. The Vietnam War wrought a profound change in America's self-image.

And then as Vietnam ended came Watergate. At the worst possible time came "enemy lists" and break-ins to a doctor's files. Wire tappings and secret tapings of White House conversations. F.B.I. wrongdoing. Aides purportedly willing to murder if ordered to do so. Crime in the White House and huge payoffs. Americans knowing their President was a party to a felonious cover-up of criminal activities. And on goes the list of the White House "horrors" exposed during the second Nixon term.

Next the economy faltered. The productivity of rivals, Japan and Germany, challenged the hegemony of America, a lead which was so recently considered unapproachable. Soaring inflation plagued consumers and business alike and nothing the national government did or did not do seemed to help.

Americans are disspirited. Disillusioning events come too frequently. The nation on the eve of its 200th anniversary faces a tremendous challenge. Will Americans sink into despair, too demoralized and cynical to "keep the faith?" Or will they carry on the spirit which, recognizing America's faults past and present, seeks nevertheless to make her the perfect land.

The United States has achieved a remarkable level of productivity. It also has made outstanding contributions to the conquest of human disease and outer space. Remarkably, America's singular technical and scientific feats have been achieved in a relatively democratic self-governing land in which a large amount of individual freedom is enjoyed. Recognizing her heritage, the American people should and hopefully will, continue the effort to eradicate her problems in that spirit.

ADDITIONAL READING

Abel, Elie, *The Missile Crisis* (Philadelphia: Lippincott, 1966).

Allen, Frederick B., *Only Yesterday: An Informal History of the 1920s* (New York: Harper & Bros., 1931).

Bancroft, Hubert, *History of Mexico: 1824-1861* (San Francisco: A. L. Bancroft and Company, 1883-1888).

Beard, Charles A., *President Roosevelt and the Coming of the War 1941* (Hamden, Conn.: Archon Books, 1968).

Billias, George, *The American Revolution: How Revolutionary Was It?* (New York: Holt, Rinehart & Winston, 1965).

Boorstin, Daniel, *America and the Image of Europe: Reflections on American Thought* (New York: Meridian Books, 1960).

Boorstin, Daniel, *The Americans: The Colonial Experience* (New York: Random House, 1958).

Boorstin, Daniel, *The Genius of American Politics* (Chicago: University of Chicago Press, 1953).

Britton, Nan, *The President's Daughter* (New York: Elizabeth Ann Guild, 1927).

Brown, Dee, *Bury My Heart at Wounded Knee: An Indian History of the American West* (New York: Holt, Rinehart & Winston, 1970).

Brown, Richard M., *American Violence* (Englewood Cliffs, New Jersey: Prentice Hall, 1970).

Demaris, Ovid, *America the Violent* (New York: Cowles Book Company, 1970).

Gavin, James, & Arthur Hadley, *Crisis Now* (New York: Random House, 1968).

Goulden, Joseph, *Truth Is the First Casualty: The Gulf of Tonkin Affair: Illusion and Reality* (Chicago: Rand McNally, 1969).

Gruening, Ernest, & Herbert Beaser, *Vietnam Folly* (Washington, D. C.: The National Press, Inc., 1968).

Hacker, Andrew, *The End of the American Era* (New York: Atheneum, 1970).

Hammer, Richard, *One Morning in the War: The Tragedy at Son My* (New York: Coward-McCann, 1970).

Harvey, Frank, *Air War—Vietnam* (New York: Bantam Books, 1967).

Hersch, Seymour, *My Lai 4: A Report on the Massacre and Its Aftermath* (New York: Vintage Books, 1970).

Holand, Hjalmar, *Explorations in America Before Columbus* (New York: Twayne Publishers, 1956).

Hughes, Rupert, *George Washington* (New York: W. Morrow & Co., 1926).

Jackson, Helen, H., *A Century of Dishonor: The Early Crusade for Indian Reform* (New York: Harper & Row, 1965).

Kellum, David, *American History Through Conflicting Interpretations* (New York: Teachers College Press, 1969).

Kimmel, Husband, *Admiral Kimmel's Story* (Chicago: H. Regnery Co., 1955).

Kitman, Marvin, *George Washington's Expense Account* (New York: Simon and Schuster, 1970).

Kochan, Lionel, *The Struggle for Germany 1914-1945* (Edinburgh, University Press, 1963).

Knoll, Erwin, & Judith McFadden (Eds.), *War Crimes and the American Conscience* (New York: Holt, Rinehart & Winston, 1970).

Langer, William, & S. Everett Gleason, *The Challenge to Isolation, 1937-1940* (New York: Harper & Row, 1952).

Luthin, Reinhard, *The Real Abraham Lincoln* (Englewood Cliffs, N. J.: Prentice Hall, 1960).

Maisky, Ivan, *Who Helped Hitler?* (London: Hutchison, 1964).

McCormac, Eugene, *James A. Polk: A Political Biography* (Berkeley, Calif.: University of California Press, 1922).

Means, Gaston, *The Strange Death of President Harding* (New York: Guild Publishing, 1930).

Millis, Walter, *The Road to War: America, 1914-1917* (Boston and New York: Houghton Mifflin, 1935).

Moore, Harry H. (Ed.), *Survival or Suicide* (New York: Harper & Bros., 1948).

Peithmann, Irvin, *Broken Peace Pipes* (Springfield, Illinois: Charles C Thomas, 1964).

Perkins, Whitney, *Denial of Empire* (Leyden, Netherlands: A. W. Sythoff, 1962).

Randall, James G., *The Civil War and Reconstruction* (Lexington, Mass., Heath, 1969).

Randall, James G., *Lincoln, the President* (New York: Dodd, Mead & Co., 1945).

Ruiz, Ramon, *The Mexican War—Was It Manifest Destiny?* (New York: Holt, Rinehart & Winston, 1963).

Schell, Jonathan, *The Military Half* (New York: Knopf, 1968).

Sheehan, Neil, Smith, Hedrick, Kenworthy, E. W., & Fox Butterfield, *The Pentagon Papers* (New York: Bantam Books, 1971).

Sloane, Irving, *Our Violent Past: An American Chronicle* (New York: Random House, 1970).

Spock, Benjamin, & Mitchell Zimmerman, *Dr. Spock on Vietnam* (New York: Dell Publishing Co., 1968).

Stampp, Kenneth (Ed.), *The Causes of the Civil War* (Englewood Cliffs, New Jersey: Prentice Hall, 1965).

Stowe, Leland, *While Time Remains* (New York: Knopf, 1946).

Stringfellow, William, *Dissenters in a Great Society* (New York: Holt, Rinehart & Winston, 1966).

Tansill, Charles, *America Goes to War* (Boston: Little, Brown & Co., 1938).

Taylor, Allan J. P., *From Sarajevo to Potsdam* (New York: Harcourt, Brace & World, Inc., 1966).

Taylor, Telford, *Nuremberg and Vietnam: An American Tragedy* (Chicago: Quadrangle Books, 1970).

Thayer, George, *The War Business: The International Trade in Armaments* (New York: Simon and Schuster, 1969).

Theobald, Robert, *The Final Secret of Pearl Harbor: The Washington Contribution to the Japanese Attack* (Old Greenwich, Conn.: Devin-Adair, 1954).

U.S. *National Commission on the Causes and Prevention of Violence,* report to the President of the United States, (Washington, D. C.: U.S. Government Printing Office, 1969).

Van Every, Dale, *Disinherited: The Lost Birthright of the American Indian* (New York: W. Morrow & Co., 1966).

Weiss, Richard, *The American Myth of Success: From Horatio Alger to Norman Vincent Peale* (New York: Basic Books, 1969).

Woodward, William E., *George Washington: The Image and the Man* (New York: Liveright, 1946).

Woolston, Howard, *Prostitution in the United States* (Montclair, New Jersey: Patterson Smith, 1969).